Contemporary Athletics & Ancient Greek Ideals

Contemporary
Athletics & Ancient
Greek Ideals

DANIEL A. DOMBROWSKI

THE UNIVERSITY OF CHICAGO PRESS

Chicago and London

DANIEL A. DOMBROWSKI is professor of
philosophy at Seattle University and the author of
several books, including *Rethinking the Ontological
Argument: A Neoclassical Theistic Perspective*.

The University of Chicago Press, Chicago 60637
The University of Chicago Press, Ltd., London
© 2009 by The University of Chicago
All rights reserved. Published 2009
Printed in the United States of America

18 17 16 15 14 13 12 11 10 09   1 2 3 4 5

ISBN-13: 978-0-226-15546-3 (cloth)
ISBN-10: 0-226-15546-3 (cloth)

Library of Congress Cataloging-in-Publication
Data
Dombrowski, Daniel A.
Contemporary athletics and ancient Greek ideals /
Daniel A. Dombrowski.
p. cm.
Includes bibliographical references and index.
ISBN-13: 978-0-226-15546-3 (cloth : alk. paper)
ISBN-10: 0-226-15546-3 (cloth : alk. paper) 1.
Sports—Philosophy. 2. Sports—Greece. 3. Sports
in literature. 4. Greek literature. 5. Greece—
Civilization. I. Title.
GV706.D65 2009
796.01—dc22
2008037225

Contents

Introduction

Everyone, even my wife, who is a recalcitrant hater of games of all sorts, acknowledges the powerful influence of athletics in contemporary society. But philosophy of athletics gets less attention than other areas of the discipline that examine the other major components of contemporary society: philosophy of religion, political philosophy, aesthetics, and philosophy of science. Perhaps the relative paucity of attention paid to philosophy of athletics is somewhat understandable in that religion, politics, art, and science are serious human pursuits, whereas, it is alleged, athletics is nonserious, playful, a mere sport or game. But the subject matter in question, athletics, is much more complex than most citizens (even fans), indeed most philosophers, have been willing to admit. I will argue that to say that athletics is nonserious is to speak a half-truth.

The thesis of the present book is that we can try to get a handle philosophically on athletics by examining it in light of several key concepts from ancient Greek philosophy: the pursuit of excellence (*arete*), the idea that the virtuous life lies in a type of moderation (*sophrosyne*), the importance of the power (*dynamis*) to both passively accept one's bodily limitations and actively try to improve one's body through athletic discipline (*askesis*), the concept of play (*paidia*), and the concept of *kalokagathia*. By this last word I intend the concept highlighted by Stephen Miller as well as by Irena Martinkova. *Kalokagathia* is derived from the Greek words for "beautiful and good," *kalos kai agathos*. The terms in this composite signify an admiration for physical and moral excellence, respectively (Miller 2004a, 247; Martinkova 2001). Either alone is insufficient.

This thesis is stated cautiously due to the methodological pluralism prevalent in contemporary attempts to understand athletics. Nonetheless, I will urge that the effort to understand and evaluate athletics in light of key Greek philosophical concepts should be seen as an equal partner along with other approaches. These other approaches include those that rely on physiology, evolutionary biology, economics (both capitalist and Marxist), psychology, sociology, anthropology, religion, linguistic analysis, and phenomenology (Lenk 1979).

After all, there is a sense in which the ancient Greeks invented athletic games and were the first to carefully examine their nature, as we will see. Further, Miller is correct to claim that there was in ancient Greece, as well as in our own day, an all-pervasive character to athletics (Miller 2004b, 104).

The first chapter of the book provides a sketch of ancient Greek athletics. Because of the painstaking work of classicists from the nineteenth century until the present (among many others who have written in English are E. N. Gardiner, H. A. Harris, M. I. Finley, Mark Golden, Nigel Crowther, Nigel Spivey, and especially Miller, and the list could easily be expanded greatly if we included German, French, and other scholars), we now have a developed idea of what ancient athletic events took place, who participated in them, where they took place, why they took place, how the victors were rewarded, and so on. Just as there are now two journals devoted to the philosophy of athletics (*Journal of the Philosophy of Sport*, many of the best articles in which have been anthologized in a volume edited by Andrew Holowchak as well as in other fine anthologies; and recently the publication of the British Philosophy of Sport Association, *Sport, Ethics and Philosophy*), so also there is now one devoted to the history of ancient athletics (*Nikephoros*). The relative paucity of attention paid to philosophy of athletics mentioned above is meant to contrast with the enormous amount of attention paid to the philosophies of religion, politics, art, and science. I do not mean to denigrate the first-rate work that has been done in philosophy of athletics over the last fifty years. This first chapter will provide both the historical background for the subsequent chapters and an introduction to the philosophical issues to be treated in the remainder of the book. But no detailed response to these philosophical issues will be offered in the first chapter.

The contemporary options before us are to be found implicitly in a spectrum of athletic contests in Homer. Should we see athletics as closer to (*a*) the informal, lighthearted games of the Phaeacians (*Odyssey*, bk. 8), (*b*) the more formal, highly competitive games commemorating the death of Patroklos (*Illiad*, bk. 23), or (*c*) the ultraserious, deadly archery contest at the end of the *Odyssey* (bk. 21)?

Classicists seem divided regarding which of these three options best captures the spirit of the ancient games at Olympia. For example, Nigel Spivey sees no need to claim that the ancient Olympic Games were instances of sublimated violence if they were themselves violent. Along with George Orwell, Spivey sees both ancient and contemporary athletics as war by other means and as exhibiting nothing less than fascist tendencies! Hence, *c* comes closest to capturing the true spirit of athletics. By contrast, Miller opts for *b* as the Homeric option that comes closest both to the spirit of the ancient Olympic Games and to what we could hope for in contemporary athletics. He seems to say that athletics could be what William James would call the moral equivalent of war.

A related question that is asked in the first chapter (but is not answered there) is whether athletics necessarily precludes a sportive sense of play. That it does not preclude a sense of play seems to be the conclusion to reach when we consider the great concern the ancient Greeks had for the fairness of athletic competition. In fact, the concept of equality under the law might very well be the greatest contribution made by ancient athletics to world civilization. In effect, we are led to ask: is it possible to take athletic events seriously without taking them too seriously? Along with Miller I will respond to this question in the affirmative.

There are three intended audiences for the book, the first two of which should be obvious on the basis of the above: both philosophers and classicists who are interested in critical appraisals of contemporary athletics. These are populations that are significantly larger, I think, than has hitherto been assumed. But there is a third audience that is really large: professionals who work in what is now called "the sports industry." Many of these are admittedly not intellectuals, but there are also many in this group who are very much interested in understanding both the history and philosophical significance of their life's work.

I will argue that the attempt to understand athletics in light of Greek philosophy can go in two different directions. In chapter 2 I will explore the first of these directions: the view of athletics as the pursuit of bodily excellence. Here I will examine the thought of the twentieth-century philosopher Paul Weiss, who can be seen as the contemporary father of philosophy of athletics. In his book *Sport: A Philosophic Inquiry* (1969) he offers a defense of what was at least implicit in the ancient philosophers, that athletics is a way of achieving *arete* through embodied means.

Weiss facilitates the effort to see athletic events as illuminating instances of general principles. The ancient Greeks, it should be emphasized, tended to be hylomorphists who gloried in both physical and mental achievement; hence they were predisposed to value highly the ideal of *kalokagathia*. By viewing athletics from afar, rather than as a participant or fan, Weiss hopes to gain Platonic insight into the role athletics could or should play in several contemporary domains, including education, the ongoing battle against sophistry, and the effort to understand the positive and negative effects of money on athletics. On Weiss's Platonic view, bodily excellence should not be denigrated even if it is not sufficient for a life well lived. Further, athletics can help us better understand the Platonic concern for being as power (*dynamis*), specifically the power to subjugate the body through athletic (or better, ascetic) discipline, on the one hand, and to nobly accept bodily limitations when the body is recalcitrant, on the other.

One difficulty is that by paying serious attention to athletics we might be seduced by the *kalos* part of *kalokagathia* at the expense of the *agathos* part. That is, the full life of a hylomorph (to be defined later) is aspirational rather than complete at any given moment. This aspiration is often derailed in athletics by an overarching desire for victory. Another difficulty is that of determining what is intrinsically valuable in athletics (its autotelic quality, on Weiss's usage) and what is instrumentally valuable, say, for the sake of character development. Regarding these and other difficulties Weiss is a helpful link between ancient Greek ideals and contemporary athletic realities, even if he is too Greek in his denigration of women athletes, as we will see.

Chapters 3 and 4 examine a different way of trying to understand athletics in light of ancient philosophical themes: sport, even the competitive sport found in athletic contests, is a type of play. The view of athletics as play rests foursquare on the ancient (especially Aristotelian) emphasis on virtue as moderation and as an avoidance of two extremes (vices) that flank it.

In chapter 3 I will consider the magisterial book of Johan Huizinga, titled *Homo Ludens* (1944), which has all of the marks of a contemporary classic. Huizinga is famous for trying to explain as much of human culture as possible by way of the ludic: athletics as well as language and philosophy, even war. This abductive project of viewing human affairs *sub specie ludi* is meant to highlight the thesis that *Homo ludens* (the human player) deserves equal footing with more well known characterizations of humans as *Homo sapiens* (the human knower) and *Homo faber* (the human maker).

It is to Huizinga's credit that he calls attention to the fact that the *Homo ludens* hypothesis is firmly rooted in Plato's philosophy, specifically in the *Laws* (803–804): God alone is ultimately worthy of seriousness and we human beings are players (in some well-known passages Shakespeare says something similar). But this does not mean that we are "merely" players in that the ludic element in us is our best feature. In this regard I will call attention to the hieratic potential of athletics. Further, the *Homo ludens* hypothesis is perfectly compatible with the agonic tendency of the ancient Greeks in that an *agon* (contest or struggle) itself is a life-affirming, albeit competitive, type of play. In our more egalitarian age we can still learn from the ancient Greeks regarding how to respond to the question of how to appropriately use our leisure time in a condition where our bodies, as well as goodness, are fragile.

In chapter 4 I will treat in detail the thought of a philosopher who has, more than any other, applied Huizinga's insights regarding play, in general, to athletics, in particular: Randolph Feezell in his recent work *Sport, Play, and Ethical Reflection* (2004a). The key insight in Feezell is that Aristotelian moderation provides the best clue we are likely to get regarding how to philosophically assess contemporary athletics.

I will defend Feezell's view that the main virtue required of an athlete, sportsmanship, ought to be seen along with other understandably well-known virtues like justice and courage. Sportsmanship is important both because of its crucial role in morally defensible athletics itself and because it is often encouraged in young people participating in team sports right at the time when they are seen as nascent moral agents. That is, sportsmanship and moral agency very often grow (or wither) together. Sportsmanship, I will argue in a Feezellian vein, is a mean between two extremes: taking athletics too seriously (the greater danger) and trivializing it. This entails a sort of attitudinal complexity in that the virtuous athlete must take athletics both seriously and nonseriously. This is in contrast to the attitudinal parsimony entailed in James Keating's view, as we will see. It is this attitudinal complexity that makes virtuous athletic participation so difficult.

Talk about athletics is frequently cheap, but it need not be so. It *does* matter how we talk about athletics, just as it matters how we talk about religion, politics, art, and science. Feezell is correct to point out that saying that a work of art is "pornography" or a "masterpiece" greatly affects how we view it. So also, to say that athletic competition is like war or business is to arbitrarily settle many of the interesting and complex philosophical issues surrounding athletics. And to say that it leads to character development is to beg the question of whether it could, in fact, do so. It is clear that participating in a hotly contested athletic event *reveals* the character of its participants (or the lack thereof), but does it build it? Feezell may very well be correct in claiming that we should expect only a mixed moral result from participation in athletics. Athletics is at once liberating and absurd. I will defend this paradoxical line of reasoning in Feezell, but only after distinguishing between the nature and the scope of the absurdity in question.

It is a mistake, I think, to assume that these two directions—athletics as pursuit of bodily excellence and athletics as play—are at odds with each other. There is more of the athletics-as-play thesis in Weiss's work than initially meets the eye, and Feezell's energetic and enormously insightful treatment of the athletics-as-play thesis is more compatible with Weiss's view that athletics is the pursuit of bodily excellence than initially seems to be the case. That is, pursuing bodily excellence through competitive sport often *is* playful, enjoyable activity engaged in for its own sake. Athletes *like* to compete in their games.

In that the middle chapters of the book are not arranged thematically, but rather in terms of three major figures in contemporary philosophy of athletics (Weiss, Huizinga, and Feezell), certain key themes will be treated in each of these three chapters: the autotelic quality of athletic competition, the problems associated with professionalism in athletics, the tension between the play element in athletic competition and the quest for victory, and so on. But these themes are not *repeated* in these chapters in that with each iteration the complexities and nuances of each of these themes will be brought to light. The purpose of these iterations is to get on the table all, or at least many of, the relevant considerations of the subject matter in question so that any conclusions reached will not be adopted hastily.

I will end the book with an emphasis on the *process* of becoming virtuous, a process that is illuminated by all of the authors treated in the previous chapters. From the above it can be legitimately inferred that the present book is a contribution not only to philosophy of athletics, but also to the renaissance of virtue ethics that has occurred in the past several decades due to the work of Alasdair MacIntyre, Philippa Foot, G. E. M. Anscombe, Rosalind Hursthouse, Peter Geach, Michael Slote, and many others. In other words, the effort to perfect ourselves as human animals is incomplete if it does not pay sufficient attention to bodily excellence. Further, because the type of virtue ethics explored in the book emphasizes the *process* of becoming virtuous, there is an obvious debt to Alfred North Whitehead and Charles Hartshorne, the major figures in twentieth-century process thought.

The aim of chapter 5 reinforces that of the book as a whole: to take what otherwise might be static ancient Greek ideals and put them in motion in contemporary athletics. The process of becoming a virtuous athlete requires several components: a dynamic version of hylomorphism that relies on, yet goes beyond, Weiss's aretism; a contemporary defense of Plotinian *askesis*, wherein the athletic roots of asceticism are uncovered; and a processual understanding of both the *Homo ludens* hypothesis and "Olympism" as defended by certain recent scholars (e.g., McNamee 2006).

As before, the key concepts from Greek philosophy that will provide the backbone to the present book are the following: *arete, sophrosyne, dynamis, askesis, paidia*, and *kalokagathia*. These ideals never were parts of a realized utopia in the ancient world, but rather provided a horizon of meaning. I will claim that these ideals still provide worthy standards that can facilitate in us a better understanding of what athletics is and what it could be (or, better, should be).

A brief apologia is in order. There are those who cynically suggest that because very few contemporary athletic figures are both excellent athletes *and* excellent people, the Greek ideals mentioned above are largely irrelevant. I offer the following reply: it is in the nature of ideals that they be lofty and difficult to exemplify without qualification. But this should not deter us.

For example, the ideal in politics, from the time of Plato until John Rawls, has been justice, but how many governments instantiate it without remainder? Despite the prevalence of injustice, however, the *ideal* of justice is still crucial in the effort to measure the degree to which actually existing states fall short of perfection. It makes a big practical difference whether we live in a society that at least approximates the Rawlsian original position or we live in an outlaw state that is entirely unjust. So also regarding the ideal of *kalokagathia*, for example. We are all ennobled by the existence of Bill Bradley, who was an excellent basketball player and still is an intelligent contributor to the polis. Even if he does not completely realize the ideal of *kalokagathia*, there is nonetheless quite a distance between him and any number of unreflective and venal athletes. We are also ennobled by Roberto Clemente's example. He was both an excellent baseball player and a humanitarian who died for the sake of others.

Clearly there is a history of using the ancient Greeks to facilitate an understanding of, or shaping of, contemporary athletics. Pierre de Coubertin, the originator of the modern Olympic Games, is especially noteworthy in this regard. I admit that there is much to admire in de Coubertin, especially his explicit statement and defense of the ideal of *kalokagathia*. But the present book resists the romantic urge found in de

Coubertin to see what the ancient Greeks said about athletics as a mysterious and authoritative sort of *Ursprache* (MacAloon 1981). Rather, because it is so difficult for us *now* to understand and evaluate athletics, it would be foolish of us to ignore the insights of the ancient Greeks, many of which are still defensible today.

Or again, because of the ancient thinkers we have a clear idea of what can be said in an intelligent way about athletics. The question is: can we improve on their ideas? In some ways, yes; and in others, no. In addition to his romanticism, other problems with de Coubertin's appropriation of the Greeks for contemporary purposes include his obvious class elitism and his sexism. Here we can do better, I think (Finley and Pleket 1976, chap. 1). The measured view I wish to defend does not include an apotheosis of the ancient Greeks. Rather, current philosophical thinking on athletics is very often *historical thinking* that relies (consciously or not) on the ancient ideals that are the foci of the present book. That is, I will be thinking *along with* the Greeks instead of looking back to them with a sort of nostalgia or syrupy sentimentalism.

Another task remains here in this preface. It is a crucial one that concerns the meaning of key terms. There is no agreed-upon technical vocabulary in philosophy of athletics. Indeed, many of the debates in the field center on the meanings of "play," "sport," "athletics," and so on, and whether "play" should be seen as the generic term under which various more specific terms should be classified.

An influential view is that of Keating, who radically separates "play" from "athletics." His argument largely proceeds on understandable etymological grounds. "Play" is derived from the Anglo-Saxon *plega* and involves the free movement of bodily exercise and the joy or delight in such movement. "Athletics," by contrast, is derived from the Greek infinitive *athleuein* and involves the effort to contend for a prize and to endure in such an effort. That is, on Keating's grounds athletics involves a competitive element that is largely lacking in play; athletics involves winners and losers that are not found in play (Keating 1964; cf. Roochnik 1975).

I confess that I used to be wholly committed to Keating's carefully argued view, but now my commitment is half-hearted. For reasons that will become apparent throughout the book (especially in the chapter devoted to Feezell's ideas), I think that a more fruitful approach is to see play as a generic category that can have (at least) three specific instances: (1) aimless play or *frolic*, from the Old High German *frolich*, which signifies a pure outburst of fun with no rules; (2) competitive, rule-governed play found in games and which in everyday discourse is called *sport* or *athletics* if the games in question test physical skill or prowess; and (3) a sort of violent play that borders on *war*. One can imagine a continuum from the outer reaches of 1 to the outer reaches of 3 that contains many shades of difference.

Further, along with William Morgan I agree that we should resist the idea that "sport" and "athletics" cannot be defined because of the multiple meanings of these terms. Morgan, relying on the middle books of Aristotle's *Metaphysics*, rightly argues against the supposed dichotomy between univocal and merely equivocal predication (Morgan 1977).

Admittedly there is a price to pay for following popular usage by treating "sport" and "athletics" as rough synonyms. First, "sport" is not derived from an ancient Greek word, as is "athletics." Because the book examines the subject matter in question from the perspective of ancient Greeks ideals, I have used "athletics" in the title for etymological rather than conceptual reasons. "Sport" would work just as well conceptually, at least as long as it was clear that by "sport" we meant competitive sporting events, rather than mere frolic. And second, the original meaning of "sport" (from the Anglo-French *disporter*, "to divert or to amuse in a pleasant pastime") seems to ally it with frolic unless it is modified by an adjective like "competitive." But a careful study of the *Oxford English Dictionary* reveals many different historical meanings of "sport" and its cognates, the most recent of which are compatible with the view of sport as *competitive* play. It seems impossible at this point to convince everyone to return to the original meaning of the term.

To sum up, I think that "athletics" and "competitive sport" are rough synonyms, but I will generally use the former because of its resonances with the ancient Greek *athleuein* and its cognates. I use this word despite the fact that in the United Kingdom and elsewhere "athletics" is reserved for track and field events; when I use the term it will refer to competitive sporting events of all sorts. (I should also note that by "soccer" I mean what most of the world means by "football." When I speak of "football," I have in mind North American football.)

My overall method can perhaps be dignified by calling it *reflective equilibrium*. This is a method made famous by Rawls and now widely used in practical philosophy. The main idea is that no one consideration is foundational or fixed in advance and that several relevant considerations must be brought into some sort of compatibility. I will return explicitly to this important method of reflective equilibrium in each chapter of the book. It is the *complexity* of athletics that makes more parsimonious methods problematic. In popular culture, for example, it is common to hear that athletics is preparation for war or merely a means to acquire capital or purely for the sake of the education of the young. And so on. Even if there is a grain of truth in each of these suggestions (I am trying to be generous here), our view of athletics would be put into disequilibrium and hence impoverished if we fixated on any one of these (see Loland 2002).

Regarding philosophy of athletics, in contrast to views of athletics prevalent in popular culture, the key considerations that must be brought into equilibrium include at least the following: (*a*) the etymology of key words as detailed in the *Oxford English Dictionary* and the Liddell-Scott *Greek-English Lexicon*; (*b*) but also the Wittgensteinian commitment to meaning as use; (*c*) first-person experience of (or phenomenology of) playing athletics, witnessing athletics as a fan, umpiring athletic events, coaching athletic teams, parenting children who play athletics, and so on; (*d*) but also an effort to objectively examine athletics from afar, say, by comparing it to other significant human actions in history, religion, politics, art, and science, including those from the Greek period. That is, by viewing contemporary athletics from the perspective of ancient Greek ideals, we can achieve some distance from our own (perhaps unexamined) assumptions.

It should be emphasized that all four of these factors are crucial; hence, to leave any one of them out is a defect, as is overemphasizing any one of them at the expense of the others. Omission or hyperbole tends to put our view of athletics into disequilibrium. Equilibrium is especially difficult to obtain because *a* is sometimes in tension with *b*, and *c* is sometimes in tension with *d*. Further, *a* and *b* together are sometimes in tension with *c* and *d* together.

This method of reflective equilibrium, most famously used by Rawls, can be traced back to Aristotle's (indeed Socrates') dialectical method. What we are trained to believe through habit (*ethos*)—a training that is very important to Aristotle—must nonetheless withstand the criticism that comes from powerful theory. The two are interdependent, although at times the person with practical wisdom (*phronesis*) must adjudicate tensions between the two (Rawls 1999a, sec. 9; Hardie 1968, chap. 3).

The complexity of athletics makes it unlikely that we would be able to adequately understand or evaluate it by means of a crisp deductive argument that starts from self-evident premises. That is, although the method of reflective equilibrium is tentative and messy, it makes up for its deficiencies by encouraging thoroughness and adequacy to the subject matter in question.

Throughout the book I will be defending what I take to be the following bold thesis: contemporary critical thinking about athletics unwittingly tends to be historical thinking. Consider three examples: (1) Although Weiss at times mentions ancient Greek ideas, it is not generally realized that just beneath the surface of his book is an ancient philosophical foundation provided by the concept of *arete*, specifically bodily *arete*. (2) Huizinga's great work deserves to be better known by contemporary scholars, yet even those who are familiar with Huizinga's work tend not to notice the ancient Greek (and medieval) core of his concept of the ludic. (3) Like Weiss, Feezell mentions Aristotle, but he does not entirely appreciate the extent to which his own view, even his Thomas Nagel–like view of athletics as absurd, is thoroughly Aristotelian.

The ultimate hope is that my integration of classical learning and contemporary philosophy will positively influence how many reflective individuals will think about athletics in the future.

The Ancient Background

I. INTRODUCTION

In this first chapter my major aim will be to provide the historical background for the subsequent chapters and to introduce the philosophical issues to be treated in the remainder of the book. But no detailed response to these philosophical issues will be offered in this chapter. Nor will I be attempting to do original historical or classical research here in that my aim, once again, is to provide *background* for the remaining chapters.

Nonetheless, my hope is that something important is going on in this initial chapter. Contemporary individuals disagree, sometimes uncompromisingly so, about the nature and significance of athletics. This disagreement is mirrored in contemporary appraisals of ancient athletics by classicists. I will be especially interested to get on the table two different views regarding ancient athletics: Stephen Miller's nuanced and generally positive assessment and Nigel Spivey's contrasting stance, which is generally skeptical, even cynical, about any effort to understand and improve contemporary athletics in light of the ancient Greek experience. Although my own sympathies are closer to Miller's than to Spivey's, the latter scholar provides a valuable service by calling into question any blithe acceptance of athletics, whether ancient or contemporary. That is, Spivey will help to keep my Miller-like optimism honest in the effort to find equilibrium among the relevant intuitions and theories concerning the nature and place of athletics in the life of a reflective individual.

2. MILLER'S MEASURED STANCE

Athletics was integral to the life of the ancient Greeks, just as it is integral to our life together today. In neither case would one do justice to the society in question if athletics were ignored. The Olympic Games were reportedly started in 776 B.C.E., in the very century when Homer is presumed to have written his epics concerning the Trojan War. Eventually games at Delphi, Isthmia, and Nemea were added to those at Olympia. The development of these stephanitic or crown games (from the Greek word for crown: *stephanos*) mirrors the development of Greek culture itself. As Miller insightfully puts the point, the fact that the Olympic Games went on even as Athens burned in 480 tells us much about Greek society (Miller 2004a, 1–4; Harris 1964, chap. 1).

It might not have been easy for Plato to give up an athletic career as a wrestler at the Isthmian Games in order to become a philosopher (Diogenes Laertius I.3.4; Spivey 2004, 32), and we can easily understand why Aristotle condescended to include a list of Olympic victors among his works (Aristotle 1984, 2.2387). When Alexander the Great spread the Hellenic world into the much wider Hellenistic one, he took athletics with him. Indeed, by the time of Alexander to be an athlete involved full-time work as what we today would call a professional. Eventually athletics became an entertainment industry among the Romans, an eventuality that sounds familiar to us today. But the ascendancy of Christianity in the fourth century C.E. brought about the termination of ancient athletics. This end was not so much the result of an antiathletics bias, on Miller's interpretation, as it was due to the fact that ancient athletics was integrally connected to polytheistic religion in that each game was sacred to some particular god or goddess (Miller 2004a, 5–7; Harris 1964, chap. 2).

We have seen that the ancient Greek infinitive *athleuein* meant "to compete for a prize"; the noun *athlon* referred to the prize itself; and an *athletes* was the one who did the competing. Although Miller knows as much as anyone about the written and visual evidence from antiquity about athletics (e.g., the various athletic artifacts in the British Museum), we will find reason to doubt his claim, based in part it seems on the etymological evidence provided by *athleuein* and its cognates, that "sport for sport's sake was not an ancient concept" (Miller 2004a, 11). I will argue that the issue is more complex than Miller admits. Who would go so far as to claim that ancient Greek athletes did not *like* to compete? In any event, herein lies the first important issue to surface in the present historical background: does athletic competition necessarily preclude a sportive sense of play? I will respond to this question in detail in due course.

It strikes us as odd today that ancient Greek athletes performed in the nude. (Miller unfortunately says "naked," which I take to have a slightly different connotation in English from "nude." Relying on a long tradition in art history, I assume that to be nude is to be bereft of clothes, whereas to be naked is to be ashamed of this fact.) The word *gymnos* meant "nude," and the verbal form, *gymnazein*, meant "to perform in the nude." A *gymnasion* was a place for nudity, specifically a place to train the body *and* the mind while nude, as we will see.

Or again, originally an *agon* was a place to watch athletic or other competition, but eventually it came to refer to the competition itself. As is well known, this word provides the basis for our word "agony." Once again, we are led to ask: is the pain (*ponos*) involved in athletic training and competition unmitigated, or do athletes *like* to train and to compete? Putting the two words together we get *gymnikos agon*: nude competitions. These were in partial contrast to *hippikos agon*, equestrian competitions, and *mousikos agon*, musical or artistic competitions (Miller 2004a, 12–14).

One of the most prominent features of ancient Greek athletics was the attention paid to the fairness of the games. It is this concern for fairness that led to separate games for men (*andres*), boys (*paides*), and an intermediate group (*ageneioi*). Curiously, there were no weight divisions, not even in events like wrestling and boxing where weight would be a major factor. But fouls were taken quite seriously. Indeed, they were punished by referees with switches (*rhabdoi*). Here we should pause. Miller insightfully would have us imagine a free man (more on women later) voluntarily subjecting himself to public flogging like a slave! In fact, he claims that "the notion of equality before the law inherent in this custom may be the most significant contribution of athletics to the ancient world" (Miller 2004a, 18). And perhaps to our world, too, we might add.

Another oddity from our contemporary standpoint, in addition to the nudity of the athletes and the lack of weight divisions, is that there were no team competitions in the stephanitic games. Perhaps the reason why this strikes us as odd is that we assume that individualism and a philosophical anthropology based on self-interest were ushered in as a result of capitalism and the rise of individual rights in the modern period, whereas the ancient Greeks, it is assumed, were more community oriented. However, in ancient athletics as practiced in the stephanitic games one-on-one competitions were the order of the day. Further, there were no prizes for second place. One person won, and all of the others lost. No doubt these practices were, at least in part, connected to the ideal of *arete*. The fact that the events involved objective criteria and tended to avoid "style points" that were at the discretion of judges only serves to highlight this concentration on the one person who achieved *arete* in a particular competition (Miller 2004a, 18–19; Finley and Pleket 1976, chap. 1).

To use the helpful language of Bernard Suits, ancient athletic events were not "performances" that required "judges" to make aesthetic decisions (as in contemporary diving competitions), but rule-governed "games" that required "referees," who acted like law enforcement officers to make sure that the rules were followed (Suits 2002, 30; Meier 2002, 52). Or again, ancient Greek athletic contests were purposive rather than artistic, although an aesthetic element could no doubt be appreciated in these purposive affairs (Best 2002; Cordner 2002).

The fact that Homer depicts athletic contests seems to indicate that these activities were already well established in his day, perhaps even dating back to the Mycenaean world. In book 23 of the *Iliad* we find the funeral games of Patroklos, and in book 8 of the *Odyssey* can be found the more informal games of the Phaeacians (also see book 5 of Virgil's *Aeneid*). In these texts we hear of footraces, wrestling, boxing, chariot racing, javelin and discus competitions, and the long jump. And we should not forget the archery competition at the end of the *Odyssey*, where athletic competition blends in with war. Although Homer's athletes did not compete in the nude, and although prizes were awarded to those who did not finish first, there is nonetheless a great deal of continuity between these games and those that occurred at Olympia (Harris 1964, chap. 3), especially the funeral games of Patroklos.

These Homeric games nonetheless leave undecided philosophic questions regarding what athletics is or should be. Clearly the archery competition at the end of the *Odyssey* is meant to settle the political question regarding who should have the power to rule over Ithaca. By way of contrast, the "pickup" games (this helpful phrase is from Miller) of the Phaeacians seem to indicate that ancient athletic competition was nonetheless compatible with relaxation, as even Miller admits, despite his aforementioned claim that sport for sport's sake was alien to the ancient Greeks. Between these two extremes lie the more formal games at Patroklos's funeral. Even here, however, there seems to be the idea of the joy of competitive sport, "a reaffirmation of life in the face of [Patroklos's] death" (Miller 2004a, 20–27; 2004b).

Whatever the appropriate contemporary philosophic appropriation of ancient athletic events might be, we are in any case rewarded by thinking through their athletic experiences. On the one hand, we are shocked to find that one of the prizes (*athla*) at the funeral games of Patroklos was nothing less than a human being, a woman; on the other, we are gratified to learn that there is no evidence of gambling by spectators over who the victor would be. As Miller puts the point, "A man might gamble on his own skill or his own *arete*, but not on that of another. Each man has something to say about his own performance, but he will not trust another man and has no faith in another's *arete*" (Miller 2004a, 28–30).

The fact that the ancient Greeks marked the passage of time in terms of the Olympic Games, rather than the other way around, is further evidence of the pervasive influence of athletics. The running events that took place every four years at Olympia included the *stadion* (about a two-hundred-meter sprint); the *diaulos* (a double *stadion*, back and forth rather than a straight four-hundred-meter stretch); a long distance race (several kilometers) called the *dolichos*; and the *hoplitodromos*, or a race with armor, shields, and helmets. The link to military training is clear in this last event, but not necessarily in the others, on Miller's view. Elaborate devices (e.g., the *hysplex*) were invented to make sure that some runners did not leave earlier than others so as to help to preserve the objectivity of victory for the winner, especially in the sprints, where close finishes were to be expected. We should also note that, on Miller's interpretation, the *stadion* was the premier Olympic event. In fact, because each Olympics was named after the winner of the *stadion*, we still know the names of 250 ancient sprinters (Miller 2004a, 31–44, 126; Harris 1964, chap. 4).

It is widely assumed in popular culture today that one of the races in the ancient Olympic Games was the marathon, supposedly first run by Pheidippides from Marathon to Athens to declare the Greeks' victory over the Persians. "But it is clear that the original 'marathon' never happened" (Miller 2004a, 46) and that the marathon was not an ancient athletic event. Harris even goes so far as to suggest that a twenty-six-mile race would have violated the ancient Greek virtue of *sophrosyne*, or "moderation": Nothing in excess! (Harris 1964, 76–77; Finley and Pleket 1976, 5).

The nonracing events included wrestling (*pale*), where opponents were not "pinned," as in contemporary wrestling, but were thrown to the ground after an initial standup position. Three falls meant that one had lost the match. Whereas Hermes was the patron god of runners and pentathletes, Herakles was worshipped by wrestlers and boxers. The *pyx*, or "boxing," was controversial in the ancient world, just as it is in our own, due to the injuries that athletes received. The boxing "gloves" used (*himantes*) were merely leather strips that did nothing to soften the blow to one's opponent. Victory was declared when one boxer either would not continue (say, by running away) or could not continue (due to serious injury or death). The *pankration* was even worse in that it blended wrestling and boxing and various other sorts of attack. Only biting and gouging were prohibited. That is, kicking and wrenching the opponent's ear or ankle were perfectly legitimate (Miller 2004a, 46–60, 184; Harris 1964, chap. 4; Finley and Pleket 1976, chap. 3). Later we will consider the philosophical issues raised by the *pyx* and the *pankration*, issues that relate to the limits of athletic play and the point at which the violence sometimes involved in athletics deserves moral disapprobation.

The ancient Olympic Games also included the pentathlon, which resulted in a single winner from among five competitions. These were the *stadion*, the *pale*, the discus (*diskos*) throw, the javelin (*akon*) throw, and the long jump (*halma*). Ancient vase painters especially enjoyed the pentathlon; and the *diskobolos* (discus thrower), in particular, was a favorite of sculptors due to the dynamic tension exhibited by this athlete as he was coiled to throw. The discus competition was much like its contemporary counterpart, except that the disks weighed progressively more with each succeeding throw. But the long jump involved several curious features: the use of a flute player to establish one's rhythm before the jump, a set of hand weights (*halteres*) that were thrown forward so as to propel one through the air in midflight, and others. And the javelin was equipped with something like a leather sling worn on the hand so as to throw the javelin properly. Surprisingly, we do not know how the overall winner of the pentathlon was decided, given the fact that the winner would presumably have won only some of the five events and lost some of the others (Miller 2004a, 60–74; Harris 1964, 77–80).

Horse races were a popular part of ancient athletics. Because horses were expensive (then as now), these events were the special provenance of the wealthy, although the charioteer was usually a slave or a hired driver. The winner, however, was the person who owned the horses rather than the horses themselves or the charioteer. Some questions come to mind at this point: what sort of *arete* is exhibited by merely owning horses, and is there any athletic ability involved in driving a chariot if it is the horses themselves who are the real athletes? Responses to these questions will inform what can be said regarding analogous issues in contemporary athletics regarding team owners, on the one hand, and athletic events (or "athletic" events?) like horse and car racing, on the other (Miller 2004a, 75–82).

As before, the Olympic Games were not just one small part of ancient Greek culture; they were an integral component of it. Olympia had important temples dedicated to Zeus, Hera, and Hestia (the goddess of the hearth). Inside the Temple of Zeus was the famous gold and ivory statue of Zeus by Pheidias. It was perhaps the most magnificent work of sculpture in the ancient world. On Zeus's right hand stood Nike, the goddess of victory. Extravagance or an understandable monument to athletic accomplishment? In responding to this question we should notice once again that ancient Greek athletic events were not seen as ancillary to the really big issues in life. At Olympia it was victory itself that was celebrated, including but not limited to athletic victory. There were stringent rules enforced to prevent bribery of referees or athletes so that the victories attained would not be tainted (Miller 2004a, 87–92; Finley and Pleket, chap. 4).

The Pythian Games, second in importance to those at Olympia, were dedicated to Apollo and took place at Delphi, specifically at the foot of Mount Parnassus, at the spot the ancient Greeks believed to be the navel (*omphalos*) of the world and the most sacred place on earth. The sacredness of the spot made the Pythia herself oracular. She was inspired by either breathing the fumes that came from a chasm in the ground or eating the leaves from nearby laurel trees. The famous inscription "Nothing in excess!" which served as the motto for ancient Greek culture in general, was found in her Apollonian temple. Once again, we should be impressed with the centrality of athletics in the ancient Greek world. Even without the fumes or the hallucinatory laurel leaves, a contemporary visitor cannot help but be awestruck by the magnificence of Delphi.

The Isthmian Games took place at the neck of land that joins the Peloponnesian Peninsula to the rest of Greece. They were sacred to Poseidon, the god of the sea. The last of the stephanitic games, again dedicated to Zeus, were at Nemea, which was the mythological site of Herakles' battle (actually a wrestling match) with a lion. These four games constituted a cycle, or *periodos*, something of an ancient Grand Slam (Miller 2004a, 95–112).

These stephanitic games were big affairs filled not only with religious awe, but also with pageantry, spectacle, or with what we today would call Super Bowl or World Cup "hype." For example, in preparation for the Olympic Games athletes would arrive about a month early at a nearby town named Elis, an ancient and literal "Olympic Village," on Miller's rendering. This period was protected by the *ekecheiria*, a sacred truce that enabled participants and spectators to travel safely throughout Greece without fear of attack. That is, there was a highly organized infrastructure that supported the games. Weaker athletes were winnowed out during this preparatory month, and the remaining athletes had to take a sacred oath attesting their competitive purity (cf. contemporary impurity brought about by steroid use). When the time for the games arrived, the athletes would participate in a procession to Olympia itself, where they would be sprinkled with the blood of a sacrificial pig and then be cleansed with water in a ritual purification at a spring named Pieria. Meanwhile the referees had to swear that they would not accept bribes (Miller 2004a, 113–122; Harris 1964, chap. 7).

The religious zenith of the games was the sacrifice of oxen at the Temple of Zeus. This provided the food for the great banquet for all in attendance. But it is hard not to think that the spectators primarily came for the games. The athletes would make a grand entrance in front of the fans through a tunnel (*krypte esodos*), passing from darkness into the light of the public area to the roar of the crowd. As Miller aptly puts the point, "The moment is dramatic—and magical. Athlete and spectator transcend their usual selves. For a few moments everyday life is left behind" (Miller 2004a, 126). Contemporary athletes and fans do not have to try hard to recreate this magic in their mind's eye. It is, to use Michael Novak's phrase, "the joy of sport," pure and simple (Novak 1976).

Part of de Coubertin's legacy was to convince many people that the purest competitive games are practiced by amateurs, those who literally love their games, from the French word for one who loves. Further, it is often assumed that those who get paid for athletic activity do not love the activity, but engage in it solely for the monetary reward. Further still, it is assumed by many that ancient Greek athletes were rewarded only with an olive wreath for their victories; hence, their activity was not sullied by mammon. But the reality of ancient athletics was much more complex than this simple picture (actually a caricature) indicates. First, even in the stephanitic games winners received not only ribbons, palms of victory, and leafy crowns (all of which are compatible with the myth of ancient athletic amateurism in the sense of nonpaid participation), but also a free meal once a day for the rest of their lives. This was quite a significant reward, especially when it is considered that multiple winners would get a free meal once a day for life for each victory. We can easily imagine multiple winners selling away some of their culinary benefits. Finally, stephanitic winners were rewarded with an *eisalasis*, a triumphal entry into their home city (Miller 2004a, 122–123, 127–128).

Second, in addition to the stephanitic games there were chrematitic games at Epidauros (the *Asklepeia*), Athens (the *Panathenaia*), Larissa (the *Eleutheria*), Sparta (the *Karneia*), and elsewhere. *Chremata* was the ancient Greek word for money. At these money games the victors (and others) actually received cash or some other type of wealth, like a valuable amphora filled with even more valuable olive oil. Miller has a complex formula for converting winnings in these chrematitic games into contemporary American dollars. The conclusion is that ancient athletes could become quite wealthy, even millionaires, especially as a result of the chrematitic games, but also as a result of multiple victories in the stephanitic games as the free meals kept piling up (Miller 2004a, chap. 7). The issues that we are led to think about today are obvious: How much financial reward for athletic prowess is enough? Does getting paid for athletic competition necessarily ruin it, or at least strip it of its play element? And what should the relationship be between "amateur" and "professional" as these terms are used today?

Quite apart from the financial benefits of the chrematitic games, there were some notable differences in the games themselves, which included boat races, an accuracy component to the javelin throw (which pushed this event closer to a military function), some team events, and a torch race that has a very distant connection to the contemporary transport of the Olympic flame. In addition, the chrematitic games often rewarded athletes who did not finish in first place (Miller 2004a, chap. 7).

It is not surprising that there is a great deal of sexism evident in ancient Greek attitudes toward women, in general, and toward women in athletics, in particular. With the exception of certain priestesses (and female charioteers disguised as males), grown women were not to be found at the Olympic Games. There are nude images of women that come down to us from antiquity, but not in athletic events. Miller and Harris nonetheless indicate that the issue is more complicated than it seems initially. There are the mythological character of Atalanta, who raced and wrestled; the physical prowess of the all-female tribe named the Amazons; the physical education of women in Sparta, which inspired the same in book 5 of Plato's *Republic* and elsewhere; and the lesser known "games of Hera" that involved female participants. Like oil and water, however, women and athletics generally did not mix (Miller 2004a, chap. 8; Harris 1964, chap. 9). As the present book proceeds we will be on the lookout for how to improve philosophically on this sorry state of affairs (Scanlon 2002, chap. 4–7; Spivey 2004, 117–121).

The ancient Greek athletes who were lionized were males, but they were not necessarily heroes. "Hero" was a technical term in ancient Greece that referred either to someone who had at least one divine parent (e.g., Herakles) or to someone who achieved a semidivine status. Further, an ancient hero had to be dead before a hero cult could arise. Not even the most famous ancient Greek athlete, Milo of Kroton, was a hero. But he was the stuff of legends: a wrestler and strongman who performed Olympic and other athletic feats of Ruthian proportions. Unlike attitudes toward women and athletics, ancient Greek attitudes toward star athletes perhaps deserve a greater contemporary hearing. The Greeks had no admiration for athletes who failed in other aspects of life or in later life. Miller quotes Pausanias as claiming that those who gloried in their strength alone were doomed to perish (Miller 2004a, chap. 9; Harris 1964, chap. 5; Finley and Pleket 1976, chap. 6). Once again, the goal was *kalokagathia*: bodily *and* moral or intellectual excellence. No doubt many ancient Greek athletes fell short of this ideal. It is by no means clear, however, that it is a good thing to abandon the goal altogether, as we will see.

The seriousness of ancient athletic competition might lead some to wonder: did the ancient Greeks ever engage in noncompetitive sport or in simple recreation? The visual evidence leads Miller to respond to this question in the affirmative. For example, hunting evolved into a pastime for the wealthy (even if fishing remained hard work in that fish were a staple in the ancient Greek diet). Acrobatics was popular, but despite the fact that *gymnos* is the root for our word "gymnastics," there were no activities that resembled contemporary gymnastics. Children are depicted juggling and playing on a seesaw, rolling hoops, and doing tricks with yo-yos. Further, playing with dice or knucklebones was common, as was playing with balls, although there is little evidence that the ancient Greeks had anything like our contemporary ball games (Miller 2004a, chap. 10). The relationship between the serious and the nonserious in the world of athletics, and the question of whether athletic competitions are nonetheless a type of play, will occupy a good deal of the present book.

The centrality of athletic competition in ancient Greek culture is evidenced in the fact that every city-state had a *gymnasion*, and some had several. In addition, it was common to have a separate wrestling building called a *palaistra*, from the ancient Greek word for wrestling, *pale*. The *palaistra* was also used for boxing and the *pankration*. Typically there was a central pit in the *palaistra* surrounded by colonnades, behind which there were bays (*exedrai*) that held classes in philosophy, rhetoric, and other disciplines. As Miller puts the point succinctly, "The fundamental feature of the palaistra-gymnasion [is that it] is a place where the mind as well as the body is exercised and trained" (Miller 2004a, 177). That is, those contemporary scholars who want to separate entirely the academic world from the athletic one are ironically at odds with the original Academy of Plato and the Lyceum of Aristotle, arguably the first two institutions of truly higher learning in world history. Admittedly the *gymnasion* was more specifically a place for physical exercise than the *palaistra*, but it is clear that the *palaistra-gymnasion* complex was a place for training in general: physical *and* mental (Miller 2004a, 176–179; Harris 1964, chap. 8; Finley and Pleket 1976, chap. 7).

It is quite understandable why many scholars are scandalized by the perversion of the intellectual life caused by runaway athletic departments in contemporary American universities and similar perversions elsewhere. The legacy from the ancient Greeks, however, seems to be that the best way to deal with this problem would not be to give in to a Cartesian view of the human person wherein body and mind (or soul) are seen as two radically different substances and hence need radically different training programs. Rather, the Greeks tended to be hylomorphists who saw the material part of a human being (*hyle*) as integrally connected to, as informed by, the structure (*morphe*) given to it by mind (or soul). This hylomorphism was crucial in the effort to achieve the ideal of *kalokagathia*. Not only Aristotle, with his obvious hylomorphism, but also Plato would have been committed to this ideal. That is, it would be anachronistic to view Plato as a Cartesian in this regard in that the Academy itself was a *gymnasion-palaistra* complex that was the site of both bodily and intellectual training. For some curious reason this is one of the best-kept secrets in the history of ideas. But seeing the Academy in this way makes sense if human beings themselves are, to coin a word, "soulbodies" or "mindbodies" rather than souls or minds radically separate from bodies.

Of course the biggest danger for historians, in general, and historians of philosophy, in particular, is anachronism. Hence, we might feel a bit skittish in thinking that Plato's Academy and Aristotle's Lyceum were something like contemporary North American college campuses. But Miller seems to suggest that there might not be as wide a gap as we might initially suppose between contemporary academic life in North America and that in antiquity: "Both gymnasia were in Athens: the Akademy at the northwest of the city, and the Lykeion to the east. In both cases we should envision something like a college campus with areas of trees and grass surrounding the buildings—the palaistra and the gymnasion. . . . The total area of these sprawling suburban schools is not known, but the Akademy has been estimated at about 180,000 square meters" (Miller 2004a, 184–185). On a Platonic and Aristotelian basis, the key question seems to be how exactly to calibrate the proper balance between physical and intellectual training.

The personnel involved at a *gymnasion* included the *gymnasiarchos* (the leader of the *gymnasion*), the *paidonomos* (the leader's assistant), and *paidotribai* (physical trainers). These last were considered inferior to those who taught reading and writing, but superior to those who taught military skills, which were not seen as identical to athletic skills. It must be admitted, however, that part of the two-year training period (the *ephebeia*) for young men about to become citizens took place in the *gymnasion* and involved some specifically military skills.

The evidence from Plato's *Lysis* (where the character Socrates is led into the *palaistra* by a group of young men) and other dialogues indicates that the nudity of the trainees led to homoerotic passion on the part of some individuals; hence, some city-states prohibited homosexuals from entering the *gymnasion-palaistra* for fear that they would corrupt the youth. The Romans as well tended to be suspicious of nudity in athletics at least in part due to this concern (Miller 2004a, 184–185, 201; Harris 1964, chaps. 6, 8; Finley and Pleket 1976, chap. 7). The issue of homosexuality in ancient Greek athletics is a complex one that should at least be acknowledged, but it will not be my focus in this book (Scanlon 2002, chaps. 3, 8–10).

Some graduates of the *gymnasion* went on to what we today would call professional careers in athletics. By the Roman period athletes "were professional in every sense of the word," according to Miller (2004a, 207). This judgment is doubtful if at least one meaning of the word refers to literally making a *professus*, as in a religious profession of vows, to take some lofty, otherwise supererogatory ideal, and voluntarily make it a duty. Presumably what Miller has in mind, by contrast, is that athletes in the Hellenistic and Roman periods got paid for their athletic activities and did not engage in "competition for its own sake" (Miller 2004a, 207; Reid 2006a). As before, however, the issue is complicated and hence will not be resolved here in the first chapter of the book.

Nonetheless, I would like to offer a preliminary example to indicate some of the complex factors involved in judgments regarding amateur and professional. Unlike Socrates (*Apology* 19E), I am a professional philosopher in the sense that I get paid to teach philosophy and to read and write as a philosopher. I do not get paid a great deal, but certainly enough to live well. But at the same time I am an amateur in the sense that I love what I do and wake up every morning with a Bergsonian élan vital and a bounce in my step as I go to "work." I would philosophize even if I were not paid to do so; indeed, for many years I (along with many others) willingly studied philosophy without pay. Hence, my being a professional philosopher does not strike me as being at odds with philosophizing "for its own sake." It is unclear to me why something analogous could not obtain for paid athletes who love their sport. At one point Miller comes close to this judgment when he notes that "amateur" and "professional," both of which have Latin rather than Greek roots, might ultimately be compatible. That is, money does not *necessarily* ruin athletics (Miller 2004a, 212).

But perhaps because of the conjunction of professionalism and specialization, athletes in antiquity were sometimes, and perhaps legitimately, characterized as "dumb jocks," to use the contemporary phrase. For example, the noted medical author Galen held that athletes were often deficient in reasoning powers to the point where they only had the intellectual capacity of pigs. Philostratos and Xenophanes echo this sentiment. These negative judgments seem to be the result of *too much* money given to athletes, which led to a sort of intellectual and moral sloth (all three of these authors are quoted in Miller 2004a, 208–215, 218; 2004b).

Athletic games generally served a positive role in ancient Greek culture. They may well have been what William James hoped they would be: moral equivalents or substitutes for war (James 1984). They promoted pacific communication across otherwise bellicose city-state borders. At times, however, political strife was fostered as a result of athletic competition. It does not surprise us today that political factors, as well as economic ones, can have a corrosive effect. For example, leaders in Syracuse were infamous for trying to lure away good athletes from other cities to compete for them. There was no escaping the fact that ancient athletes (not to mention their contemporary counterparts) were seen as proxies for their native land. Overall, however, Miller (correctly, I think) puts the relationship between politics and ancient athletics in positive terms:

> It should not surprise us that politics, and even occasional violence, played a part at the games. What is more surprising is that the episodes were so infrequent, and that the games went on nonetheless. The Olympic Games of ancient Greece lasted for more than a millennium, and they were never canceled. In 480, with the Persians on the doorstep, the games went on. . . . The modern Olympics are just over a century old. In that time one was almost destroyed by murder (Munich, 1972), and three by major boycotts (Montreal, 1976; Moscow, 1980; and Los Angeles, 1984), all for political motives. And the games of 1916, 1940, and 1944 did not go on at all because of the political situation. Perhaps we do need to study ancient practices more closely, after all. (Miller 2004a, 225; Finley and Pleket 1976, chap. 8)

Although judgments regarding the relative worth of athletic competition, whether these judgments be positive or negative, are clearly open to dialectical criticism, the pervasiveness of both ancient and contemporary athletics in their respective cultures is not open to question. Tracing the influence athletics had (or has) on literature, art, and philosophy would be an enormous task; the present chapter only scratches the surface in this regard. For example, athletic metaphors are legion in Plato and Aristotle, as when Protagoras complains that Socrates' criticisms made him dizzy because they were like the blows of a powerful boxer (*Protagoras* 339E). Here we are led to realize that Socratic dialectic, like a boxing match, is a type of *agon*. As Karl Popper often noted, criticism is the lifeblood of both philosophy and science, such that both disciplines would wither without its influence (Popper 1979). Or again, we have seen Miller emphasize the fact that the equality before the law (*isonomia*) that is the necessary condition for democracy was originally an athletic notion: winners were to be determined according to objective criteria, rather than through ancestral lineage, and so on, and those who violated the rules were to be punished regardless of their social status. Miller is also astute to alert us to the fact that when Socrates ironically proposed in the *Apology* (36D–E) that he be given free meals for life for the services his dialectical criticism provided for Athens, he was merely asking that he be treated with the respect due to a victorious Olympic athlete (Miller 2004a, 232–234).

We know that at least some victorious ancient athletes were also good men, as was the famous boxer Diagoras of Rhodes. That is, it was possible to achieve athletic *arete* without succumbing to what amounted to an occupational hazard for successful athletes: the sin of hubris or pride. Although Aristotle goes out of his way to indicate that it is a mistake to overemphasize bodily education in the manner of the Spartans (*Politics* 1337A–1339A), his own Lyceum, along with Plato's Academy, was a place for bodily exercise. Indeed, Miller indicates that the best-preserved portrait of Plato has him wearing the ribbon of an athletic victor (Miller 2004a, 235–240).

3 · SPIVEY'S CHALLENGE

The tenor of Spivey's approach to athletics is evidenced in his account of its origins in the period before the eighth century B.C.E., the time when the Olympic Games started. Although the earliest identifiable deities worshipped at Olympia were various earth and agricultural goddesses (hence, the first great temple at Olympia was dedicated to Hera), eventually the celebration of Zeus and other gods associated with speed and physical prowess dominated. As Pausanias noted in the second century

C.E., Olympia became a "Panhellenic" sanctuary that was a showcase for all things Greek. A plurality of mythical traditions was celebrated at Olympia, among which were the twelve labors (*dodekathlon*—perhaps a better translation would be "twelve athletic feats") of Zeus's son Herakles, including his cleansing of the stable of Augeas (who was the mythical king of Elis, the nearby "Olympic Village"). This labor resonates well with the chariot races that Spivey sees as the most important and prestigious events of the Olympic Games. Spivey makes this claim despite the facts that each Olympics was named after a sprinter and that chariot racing was added to the Olympic Games later than the sprints (Spivey 2004, 86, 220, 230, 236–237).

Another myth related to chariot racing takes us to the heart of Spivey's approach. One of the most sacred sites at Olympia was the Pelopeion, the supposed tomb of Pelops. The myth was that Pelops wished to wed Hippodameia (whose name means "subduer of horses"), but her father, King Oinomaos, required that any suitor first prove himself in a chariot race. The suitor was allowed a head start, accompanied by Hippodameia, but if Oinomaos caught up with the suitor he was permitted to kill the suitor via a spear in the back. Oinomaos, it turns out, had collected the skulls of previous losers. However, because Hippodameia loved Pelops, she fixed the race by having her father's chariot compromised by replacing a bronze pin with a wax replica, which gave way in the heat of the race.

One enticing way to interpret this story is in terms of a bid not only for love, but also for kingship, a bid that was "symbolically re-enacted whenever young men competed for the 'crown' of athletic victory," according to the insightful stance of F. M. Cornford that seems to be endorsed by Spivey (Cornford 1927). Once again, *stephanos* was the ancient Greek word for crown; victory in an athletic contest allowed one to both achieve a virtual majesty and set oneself up for literally resting on one's laurels. But Spivey's take on this story has more of an edge to it than is found in Cornford's interpretation. The mythic origin of the Olympic Games lies in nothing short of violence, indeed of murder and incest (in that Oinomaos's love of Hippodameia was apparently more than that of a father for his daughter). It is this edginess that makes Spivey's approach both interesting and challenging to those who are looking for a morally defensible version of athletic competition (Spivey 2004, 125, 209–226).

At one point Spivey describes Olympia as on the fringe of pleasant, pastoral Arcadia. But his usual procedure is to disparage unbearably hot Olympia and its games. We are reminded that the hundreds of oxen killed at the feast for all in attendance at the ancient Olympic Games left the stench of hide, bones, and offal. The bovine blood that was spilled went hand in glove with the human blood that was spilled in the combat games: *pale*, *pyx*, and *pankration*. Further, he thinks that ancient athletics was brutal. Period. There is no need to see it as sublimated violence if it was in itself violent. (One wonders at this point what is violent about the sprints, the *dolichos*, the discus, the javelin, or, for that matter, wrestling.) We need to be inoculated, it seems, against those like de Coubertin who wish to whitewash ancient (and presumably contemporary) athletics (Spivey 2004, xv–xxi, 83, 250).

If Miller's view of ancient athletics seems to agree with William James's thesis regarding "the *moral* equivalent of war," Spivey's stance seems more in line with George Orwell's darker view of athletics as "war minus the shooting." Orwell thought that international athletic events were "orgies of hatred" that were devoid of a sense of fair play (James 1984; Orwell 1968). Even if there is something hyperbolic in Orwell's language, as Spivey himself admits, there nonetheless seems to be a grain of truth in Orwell's appraisal that is congenial to Spivey's stance regarding ancient and contemporary athletics (Spivey 2004, 1–4).

Both Miller (implicitly) and Spivey (explicitly) deny that the ancient Greeks and Romans had any sense of "the human player." The title of Huizinga's book, *Homo Ludens*, may be Latin, but it has nothing to do with ancient views, on Spivey's reasoning. (In due course I will contradict this claim.) In fact, Spivey goes so far as to say that in the ancient world "all games were war games" (Spivey 2004, 3). Hesiod's treatment of strife (*eris*) and toil (*ponos*), as well as Homer's treatment of the funeral games of Patroklos, are cited as evidence in favor of the idea that the will to win, especially when it includes a willingness to use guile, is an explosive phenomenon that can easily degenerate into "murderous anger" (Spivey 2004, 9). Spivey asks, "Why must the heroes . . . wrestle, race, and compete, investing so much gratuitous physical effort—except by some addictive, incorrigible habit?" (Spivey 2004, 11).

If I understand Spivey correctly, the words "addictive" and "incorrigible" are meant to be derogatory. I also suspect the same about the use of "gratuitous," but this word is especially complicated when it is realized that, in addition to athletics being gratuitous, art, philosophy, and scholarship in the classics are also gratuitous, say, when they are contrasted with a biologically necessary activity like agriculture. Further, what is Spivey's warrant for saying that *all* ancient athletic games were war games? His response seems to be that, if not on the surface in the contact games, then at least beneath the surface of the ancient *agon* was an abrasive compulsion to compete and to win that has an affinity with nothing less than Nazism (Spivey 2004, 12–13, 247–248; Mandell 1987). And Spivey is not alone in making this claim (Tannsjo 2002; Tamburrini 2002; also see Kidd 2002, 405–406). Once again, I will return to this serious charge in due course. If anything, Spivey does an excellent job of convincing us that the topic of athletics is anything but trivial!

In order to avoid the charge of hyperbole, Spivey invokes the thesis of Jacob Burckhardt that the prevailing spirit of the ancient Greeks was that of *agon* or contest. This agonic mentality lies behind not only athletic contests, but also dialectical criticism found in Plato's dialogues, theater competitions, lawsuits, the battle against nature in science, and so on. In a Burckhardt-like manner, Spivey notices that *philoneikia* (the love of competing) is barely distinguishable from *philonikia* (the love of victory). But why did the Greeks (presumably along with their contemporary fascist inheritors) love competing? Spivey seems to agree with a character in Lucian from the second century C.E. who declares that those who engage in athletic competition are out of their minds for doing so, *unless*, of course, they are understood to do so for the very practical reason that physically fit athletes were a city-state's main line of defense (Spivey 2004, 13–17). Spivey states his controversial thesis succinctly: "Ultimately there was only one intent and aim of athletic contests: to feint the stress of battle; to stay sharp and ready for war" (Spivey 2004, 18; on Lucian see Miller 2004b and Golden 2004).

Spivey himself alerts us to contrary voices from antiquity (including Euripides and Julius Caesar) who urged that good athletes do not necessarily make good soldiers. The problem Spivey wishes to solve, however, is the following one: *why* would one go to the *gymnasion* at all if not for an eminently practical reason like preparing to defend the state? But to put the issue this way clearly begs the question. That is, Spivey *assumes* that there is no joy in athletic competition, no sense of life in extremis that makes athletic competition exciting in itself quite apart from its utility. This utility could be military or perhaps medicinal, say, if one were encouraged to get some exercise by one's physician (Spivey 2004, 24–30).

The fact that going to the *gymnasion* was a civic *duty* for ancient Greek citizens, correctly emphasized by Spivey, does not in itself indicate a military duty. Rather, Pausanias tells us that a habitation without a *gymnasion* was not really a city; hence, it, along with the market (*agora*) and the council house (*bouleuterion*), was a social institution, specifically a *retreat* from economic and political affairs, as Spivey notices. Very often the antidotes for Spivey's excesses are to be found in his own admissions. Despite the fact that Spivey sees the *gymnasion-palaistra* complex as a retreat, he oddly refers to the wrestling that went on there as combat, which seems to collapse wrestling into the full-contact activity of the *pankration*. It also seems to contradict the third-century-C.E. treatise *On Gymnastics* written by Philostratos. Or again, the fact that the Greeks encouraged both bodily and intellectual fitness (i.e., *kalokagathia*) does not legitimate Spivey's saying that such was primarily military fitness (Spivey 2004, 31–33, 37, 56–69; on Philostratos see Miller 2004b and Golden 2004).

It seems to me that Spivey would have been better served to see ancient athletics as part of the life of moderation (*sophrosyne*), between exclusive concern for the bodily and exclusive concern for the intellectual. He does notice the balance, symmetry, and measured proportions of pentathletes, in particular, in contrast to lithe runners and stocky participants in the combat sports. But he quickly leaves this theme in the effort to emphasize the connection between the javelin throw and military practice (Spivey 2004, 91, 95). We have seen, however, that in the stephanitic games there was no accuracy component to the javelin throw, thereby diminishing any connection to military practice. It is nonetheless at least understandable why Spivey sees a resemblance between the javelin throw and military practice, given the use of spears by the military. But such a resemblance regarding running seems quite a stretch. Consider his view: "Running was a contest involving considerably less risk of personal injury than chariot-racing or the combat sports, but there is no evidence that it was therefore regarded with disdain. After all, the most lethal of participants in Homer's Trojan War was Achilles, whose usual Homeric epithet is "fleet-footed" (*podarkes*), and whose swift efficiency as a killing-machine was in no small measure based upon his sprinting speed . . . with a punching, piston-like movement of the arms to gain extra momentum" (Spivey 2004, 112). The idea that we should expect disdain for any athletic activity that does not risk a great deal of personal injury only makes sense against the background of Spivey's tendentious thesis. Further, to describe the runner's arms as "punching" seems contrived. If running is seen as essentially connected to military practice, why not cooking as well? Soldiers sometimes need to run, but every day they need to eat. That is, it is hard to see running and eating as necessarily connected to military practice the way the *hoplitodromos* is so connected (Spivey 2004, 115–116).

Spivey is to be thanked for reinforcing the widely held view that ancient athletics was largely restricted to the aristocratic class of males. For example, slaves were prohibited from participating in the Olympic Games. Class distinctions also enable us to see why there was no marathon run in antiquity: not only would it have violated *sophrosyne*; it also would have had negative associations with nonaristocratic messengers who ran all day. It was only members of the upper class, it was believed, who could have fully appreciated the enormous "Victory-bearing" (*Nikephoros*) statue of Zeus at Olympia, or any other statue that commemorated victory, for that matter. And Pindar's famous victory odes were presumably not the stuff memorized by those who were poor and uneducated (Spivey 2004, 114, 130, 135–165).

The purpose of the present discussion of the ancient Greek background is to provide an instructive link to contemporary athletics. Spivey is characteristically less optimistic than Miller regarding the question of whether such a link can help us today in the effort to understand, and assess positively, the value of athletics. The ancient Olympic Games were officially terminated at the end of the fourth century C.E. by the Christian emperor Theodosius I of Constantinople. Some of the concerns, then, are not unrelated to contemporary concerns about athletics: the narcissism of athletes, the uselessness or gratuitousness of athletic activity, and so on. Along with Miller, however, Spivey thinks that there was no huge intellectual chasm between early Christianity and athletics, as is evidenced especially in Saint Paul's writings, where we are encouraged to fight the good fight and to finish the race so as to receive the crown of righteousness (II Timothy 4:7). Saint Paul also thought that Jesus was the forerunner in this regard, who set the pace and carried the torch before (Hebrews 6:20). Spivey even notes that early Christian mystics were referred to as "athletes for Christ" (Spivey 2004, 202–205).

Some knowledge of ancient athletics was preserved in the medieval period, especially by those physicians who were interested in Galen, the ancient surgeon to athletes. But from the late sixteenth century until the present there have been intermittent efforts to resuscitate ancient Greek athletic ideals so as to illuminate contemporary culture. And here is where Spivey's skepticism or cynicism kicks in due to the tendency on the part of the resuscitators to romanticize ancient athletics. If the present book is successful, it will be due to conscious efforts on my part to avoid such romanticizing so as to respond adequately to Spivey's thought-provoking criticisms (Spivey 2004, 240).

Examples of efforts to revive "the Olympic spirit" are legion: in 1592 Pierre du Faur wrote the first modern dissertation on ancient athletics; in 1733 an opera on ancient athletics was written that was put to music by Vivaldi; in 1766 the ruins of ancient Olympia were rediscovered by Richard Chandler from Oxford; also in the eighteenth century the German philologist J. J. Winckelmann analyzed statues of athletes from antiquity; from the nineteenth century until the present various classicists have excavated ancient athletic sites (including Miller at Nemea); and, as we have seen, in the late nineteenth century Pierre de Coubertin brought about an Olympic renaissance that continues to this day. We have also seen that Spivey goes out of his way to make the point that in the 1930s Hitler gladly funded renewed excavation at Olympia; staged a relay conveying "the Olympic flame" from Greece to Germany; commissioned Leni Riefenstahl to make a still influential, monumental film dedicated to fascist athletics (a redundancy for Spivey?); and planned to have the contemporary Olympics permanently housed at Nuremberg in a four-hundred-thousand-seat stadium. War *with* the shooting got in the way (Spivey 2004, 238–248).

Two points remain. First, the reason why Spivey should be taken seriously is that, as he puts it, "the values of physical culture articulated in Classical Greece have conquered the modern world" (Spivey 2004, 249). Such a conquest should not go unchallenged; in Socratic fashion we should interrogate contemporary apologists for athletics so as to asymptotically approach together the truth about athletics.

Second, it should not escape our notice that as an afterthought at the end of his book Spivey makes an admission that complicates his dominant stance. He even refers to this afterthought as an "ultimate truth." The ultimate truth in question is the following: in contrast to plowing a field, athletic activity is "fun" (Spivey 2004, 250). Indeed. This afterthought on Spivey's part makes it easier than it would otherwise be to reach reflective equilibrium between Miller's and Spivey's contrasting, but not necessarily contradictory, stances.

2

Weiss and the Pursuit of Bodily Excellence

I. INTRODUCTION

Before Paul Weiss did first-rate philosophical work in aesthetics, he tried his hand at drawing, painting, poetry, playwriting, and sculpture; he also talked with composers, choreographers, actors, and painters. Before he wrote his book on athletics, he also did extensive research, but it did not include efforts to sink free throws, kick field goals, run sprints, or play golf. He takes first-person accounts of athletics seriously, but these are others' first-person accounts. Nonetheless, Weiss insightfully points out that if we are willing to admit, as surely we are, that coaches know many things that athletes do not know, then we should also be open to the possibility that reflective persons who have thought carefully about both athletics and philosophical problems might understand some things about athletics that not even coaches or sportswriters typically understand. To take an analogy from political philosophy, a king might know best about some *particular* monarchical function, but Hobbes knows more about what is *essential* to all monarchs and about what the arguments for and against monarchy might be (Weiss 1995a, 655, 658).

What the philosopher of athletics should be interested in are illuminating instances of general principles, he thinks, especially instances that may have previously been hidden or neglected. Or again, the philosopher of athletics should attend not only to experience, but to particular types of experience where philosophical ideals play a major role. In the terms of the present book, we should therefore be interested in illuminating instances of *arete, sophrosyne, dynamis, askesis, paidia,* and *kalokagathia.* These Greek ideals, in turn, often overlap with certain well-known problems in contemporary philosophy: how one ought to behave, how mind and body interact, how rules should be applied, and so on (Weiss 1995a, 656).

In this chapter we will explore Weiss's theory that athletics is best understood as competitive activity wherein young men seek bodily excellence. We will see that this theory is to a certain extent compatible with the athletics-as-play hypothesis: "There is . . . a seriousness exhibited even in the simplest and most innocent of games and play, and a freshness and spontaneity exhibited in most competitions. Both are subject to limiting conditions" (Weiss 1995a, 656). But Weiss thinks that play plays (if the redundancy be permitted) a smaller role in athletics than Huizinga and Feezell admit. It is clear that in one important respect Weiss's view is very Aristotelian, in that it is centered around the concept of excellence, or *arete.* Robert Ehman, however, detects an un-Aristotelian a priorism or abstractness in Weiss that is problematic. I will partially come to Weiss's defense in this regard (Weiss 1995a, 659; Ehman 1970).

As recently as 1995 Weiss defended the stance that we chiefly perfect ourselves as human beings by enhancing our character. This stance goes hand in glove with the trope of athletic directors and coaches that participation in athletics builds character (or at least *could* build character) by providing opportunities to accept victory and especially defeat gracefully, to be fair minded and cooperative, and so on. Athletics is unique in the possibilities it provides for character development due to the fact that it involves besouled character in a bodily way; it makes possible a "character-controlled body" (Weiss 1995a, 660).

The character of athletes is tested in the plot of an athletic contest itself, which, like Greek tragedy, involves properties like recognition and reversal. We will see that in one sense an athletic contest is even more "tragic" than Greek tragedy in that it is not known beforehand in an athletic contest who will lose (Keenan 1973; Holowchak 2002a; also Best 2002; Cordner 2002; Kaelin 2002). But in a different sense Weiss is also correct to point out that it is life itself that is *really* tragic in that it involves egregious suffering and premature death, in contrast to what goes on in an athletic contest. In due course we will also consider how Weiss's method relates to amateur versus professional games and to the issue of women and athletics.

The chapter ends with an extended Platonic excursus that is very Weissian in nature. I will show both that Plato's dialogues exhibit a wide-ranging set of beliefs concerning athletics and that the character Socrates in these dialogues by no means denigrates athletics. The aims of the chapter rely on the deceptively simple Platonic and Weissian assumption that to be an excellent athlete is not necessarily to be an excellent person, an assumption that is often contradicted in practice in the sort of society we live in at present (Carr 2002).

2. EXCELLENCE AND YOUNG MEN

I think that it is no exaggeration to say that Weiss started philosophy of athletics (or philosophy of sport) as it exists today, despite the fact that some very good articles (e.g., Keating 1964) appeared before Weiss's book on the topic was published in 1969. This accomplishment is especially odd because the first sentence of his book states, "I am not an athlete." Because of the paucity of material on the subject matter in question, Weiss had to largely proceed alone and without a compass or guide. But he did have the ancient Greek philosophers to rely on. He notes that although athletics is widely practiced, and even more widely observed, it is insufficiently understood philosophically. So it makes sense that Weiss tries to make philosophical sense of athletics in terms of some key concepts from the ancient period (Weiss 1969, vii–ix).

Weiss seldom uses the Greek word *arete*. But it is clear that the English word "excellence," which roughly translates the Greek, is at the center of his approach to athletics. Weiss is an aretic pluralist. That is, he believes human beings can be excellent in many different ways. However, his thesis is that young men, in particular, find it easier to "master their bodies" and to achieve excellence in athletics than to achieve excellence in other areas. It is extremely hard for young men to be pious or wise or to be great scientists or successful entrepreneurs. Although athletics interests almost everyone, according to Weiss, it is young men who tend to excel athletically (Weiss 1969, 3–4).

Why have philosophers tended to ignore athletics? Weiss thinks that even Plato and Aristotle did not devote sufficient attention to the topic, despite the prevalence of athletics in ancient Greek society. (But they do provide us, I will argue, with the concepts that can enable us to best understand athletics today.) One reason why the great figures in the history of philosophy have largely ignored athletics is that they have exhibited a prejudice against physical activity in contrast to intellectual activity. They have been "Platonists" in this regard, even if Plato's dialogues indicate an extensive and nuanced understanding of athletics, as we will see at the end of the present chapter. Weiss is on thin ice when he links this prejudice with a different historical prejudice against slaves and those in lower economic classes. The issue is complicated because the physical activities of ancient athletes, even of modern athletes until the late nineteenth century, were mostly performed by the relatively wealthy. To be specific, there is something misleading in Weiss's idea that "as befits the well-placed in a slave society, Aristotle and other Greek thinkers dealt mainly with what concerned the well-born," because historically athletics *has* concerned the wellborn. He is closer to the truth when he says that ancient athletes, although freemen, were thought inferior to other citizens (Weiss 1969, 6–7; Veblen 1934).

It is ironic that one contemporary philosopher who defends a view similar to Weiss's is Andrew Holowchak. His persuasive "aretism" preserves much that is of value in Weiss's stance, although it is by no means clear that one needs to criticize liberalism in order to do so. That is, there might not be as much of a connection between aretism in athletics and an opposition to liberalism as Holowchak seems to think (Holowchak 2002b, 315–317; 2004; Dombrowski 2001).

In any event, as a liberal political theorist Weiss is correct to emphasize the idea that merely because an activity is widespread is not sufficient grounds for philosophers to disparage it. "The common can be good," he insists. But what is common, on Weiss's interpretation, is athletic *spectatorship*, not first-person athletic activity. This is what enables Weiss to resist the temptation to say that athletic competition is a primal drive. People like to watch young men compete, but not necessarily to compete themselves. (Later I will argue, along with Feezell, that Weiss should speak for himself in this regard.) "Some perform exceptionally well in middle age, though these are so few in number that almost every case awakens our wonder and admiration. Most men have no athletic stature." It is fortunate for young men, however, that they have this avenue to excellence in that there is not much else they can do well. "No longer boys, they are not yet full adults, able to function as prime factors in society, state, or civilization. The best that most of them can do is to be good at sport" (Weiss 1969, 8–11).

Largely because of Weiss, one no longer has to apologize for taking a philosophical interest in athletics. If this were his only contribution to philosophy of athletics, he would deserve praise. But, in addition, he has left us with one of the most important philosophical conceptions of athletics with which those interested in this field must contend, a conception that relies heavily on Greek philosophy: the concept of bodily *arete*.

Weiss complains (mistakenly, I think) that none of the Greek philosophers discussed the nature of athletics in sufficient detail, a neglect that became the norm for subsequent philosophers. This is ironic in view of the fact that Weiss thinks that the Greek philosophers *could* have written a treatise on athletics, a treatise supplied by Weiss himself. Indeed, Weiss thinks of athletics in Greek terms in that it is a source or instance of larger truths or first principles. The interest human beings of all ages and in all walks of life have in athletics is due, according to Weiss, to a concern for bodily *arete*, or excellence (Weiss 1969, 5–8; Mihalich 1982, chap. 2).

Human beings have the ability to appreciate the excellent, and they want to share in it. The Weissian clue that reveals the essential nature of athletics as a concern for bodily excellence is the fact that it is primarily young men who are most absorbed in it. We have seen that his argument is that there are many ways in which people can become excellent (intellectually, morally, or in terms of some skill or *techne*), but young men have neither the maturity nor the experience to become excellent in these other ways, so they turn to athletics. No longer boys, but not yet fully adult men, if young men want to fulfill themselves *now* it is easiest to do so through their bodies, unless, perhaps, they are prodigies in mathematics or music or chess. Nonetheless, prodigies in these areas usually continue their excellence throughout life ("prodigy" is derived from the

Latin for "to foretell"), but in athletics one "succeeds magnificently only when he is young" (Weiss 1969, 11–12).

Achieving one's *telos* as a human being entails the Greek commonplace that one be perfected both physically and mentally: *kalokagathia*. Weiss views athletes as representatives of all mankind such that the (merely) mentally adept, like Weiss himself, can vicariously be completed human beings. The athlete gives us an idealized portrait of ourselves; the athlete is bodily excellence in the guise of a human being (Weiss 1969, 13–14, 17).

3. METHOD

There is nothing apologetic in Weiss's tone, and he offers no excuses for his method, which consists in viewing athletics from afar with very little personal experience. He points out that one who is immersed too soon in the world will too soon get lost in particularity. There is much to be gained, he thinks, in first standing away from athletics as an outsider in order to get one's bearings. When Weiss vicariously reenters the practical world of athletics, he does so armed with Greek concepts like *arete* (excellence), *eudaimonia* (happiness), *telos* (goal or fulfillment), and *dynamis* (dynamic power) (Weiss 1995a).

For example, Weiss uses Plato's famous definition of being in the *Sophist* (247E) as dynamic power (*dynamis*), specifically the power to affect others and to be affected by others, in order to explain how athletes occupy a middle position with respect to the possibilities regarding human activity and passivity. One extreme is exhibited by the "naturalistic mystic" or Stoic who passively gives up all discrimination and seeks only to be in harmony with whatever is. The other (foolish) extreme is the aggressive attempt to subjugate all realities that offer us resistance. In reality, every human action has something of both activity and passivity in it (as Kant realized), with excellence in athletics consisting in knowing when and how to subjugate one's own body or those of others, and when and how to accept one's own bodily limitations or those of others as they are (Weiss 1969, 35–36, 81). Despite Weiss's lack of first-person experience as an athlete, his Platonic observations here ring true.

Or again, the athlete and coach learn the art of actively strategizing, without which one passively leaves the outcome of a game to the opponents or to luck. The athlete learns proper roles in athletic competition by determining when to receive and give and wherein lie relevant rights and duties. One cannot live a life solely of the mind for very long; hence, athletics offers a convenient agency for unifying human beings. Training (*askesis*) not only allows one to accept one's body as oneself, but also to actively habituate the body properly. But there is not only the danger of leading a life that is too intellectual: the athlete, who comes to accept the body as the self, runs the opposite risk of giving up altogether the attempt to allow the mind to dwell on objectives that are not germane to what the body is. Weiss's hope is that a coach could be more than a drill sergeant, that a coach could be a model human being or a sage who could help athletes lead lives of *sophrosyne*, or "moderation" (Weiss 1969, 41, 46, 50–51, 86–94, 161).

If we do not take it to be our main task to have athletes become excellent, we come to treat them as workers or as appendages. The body is to be accepted, but only subject to conditions that seek excellence. Athlete and thinker, according to Weiss, differ only in the relative attention they give to body and mind, respectively. The thinker inevitably unites in some fashion with his or her body, but largely passively so, such that bodily influences are not exactly within the thinker's control. That is, the thinker's acceptance of body is often attenuated (Weiss 1969, 53).

Weiss is intent on defending the claim that the athlete is not wasting time, even if the athlete does not achieve a full life. It will always be noble work to become a body, to direct the body toward a realizable end. Of course athletes often fall short of their noble ideals, as do philosophers (think of the career of Martin Heidegger), but, as we will see when we consider Feezell, athletics may be just as important in its ability to *reveal* character (or lack thereof) as in its ability to *build* it. For example, young athletes (almost a redundancy for Weiss) tend to be easily tempted by praise and often have conceit parade as self-confidence. Further, it is not easy to return to the anonymity of the undramatic everyday world once one's athletic career is over (Weiss 1969, 19, 21, 30, 84–85, 99; Feezell 2004a). Weiss's view is captured in the following:

An athlete can . . . be treated as offering one step in a progress toward the state of being a full, matured, i.e., a completely healthy, man [sic]. Having achieved a bodily excellence, the athlete can go on to try to master the other dimensions of himself, and so eventually become excellent on every side. Occasionally we hear of men who have done this. But for most it is more than enough to achieve the state of being excellent in some more limited area. For the young man there is nothing he is likely to do as well as make himself be an excellent functioning body. And there is hardly a better opportunity for doing this than that provided by contests and games. (Weiss 1969, 99)

Much of Weiss's thought on athletics consists in relating his concept of excellence to (and sometimes forcing it on, given his lack of first-person experience as an athlete) the phenomena. For example, a race or an endurance contest is designed to show one aspect of "the best" in human beings because these contests show them up against the limits of exhaustion; likewise, athletic contests that test accuracy pit human beings against an implacable, powerful nature; public athletic events and team sports are meant to expose defects in character that might not be noticed in private; professional athletes run the risk of degenerating into mere entertainers when they are no longer engaged in the task of building character; colleges that, in effect, become "farm teams" for professional athletics run the danger of perverting themselves; perfection is a consequence of athletics only when properly pursued; and so on. Both the scholar and the athlete are directly related to that finality called "actuality" by Weiss, with the athlete constituting a localized version of perfection not always inferior to that attained by the mathematician (Weiss 1969, 121, 130, 168, 206–209, 244, 247).

Paul Kuntz is correct in noting that by "philosophy of sport" Weiss means an account of athletics as it reveals a human being's encounter with the four modes of being in Weiss's metaphysics, modes that are largely derived from Plato and Aristotle: existence, actuality, the ideal, and God. Obviously the tension between existence and actuality, on the one hand, and the ideal (of excellence), on the other, constitutes the core of Weiss's theory. But Kuntz notices in his reading of Weiss's *Philosophy in Process* that the athlete is at least implicitly religious in bodily reliance on someone or something outside of the athlete's control that enables the athlete to continue to pursue excellence; however, one cannot expect the *cosmos* to always make things right for the athlete. In any event, Kuntz is correct to alert us to Weiss's belief that the excellent athlete, who takes both mind and body seriously, is Plato's state in the *Republic* writ small; the excellent athlete is also the embodiment of justice (*dike*) and moderation (*sophrosyne*) in Aristotle's uses of these terms (Kuntz 1976, 1977; Weiss 1969, 190; 1971).

We have seen that it is significant that the first words of Weiss's groundbreaking book *Philosophy of Sport* are "I am not an athlete" (Weiss 1969, vii). Although he thinks that he has not ignored entirely a first-person singular approach to athletics, his account is largely an effort to chart the new territory in philosophy of athletics in terms of the Greek concept of *arete*. Although he at least considers the view that athletics or sport is primarily rooted in play, he is drawn more forcefully toward the Greek view that athletics is first and foremost part of an overall search for excellence (Weiss 1995a, 658). In this regard Weiss is close to Miller and Spivey and seemingly far removed from Huizinga and Feezell.

It should be noted here that Weiss is rightly concerned with the bodily excellence of human beings. This is in contrast to the "transhuman" athletic goods defended by some contemporary scholars, who are ably criticized by Mike McNamee (McNamee 2007). Transhumanists glory in the alleged fact that blood doping and steroids are only the tip of the iceberg. Transhuman excellence, fueled by cutting-edge medical technology, in contrast to the human excellence treated by Weiss, will eventually enable athletes to approximate the feats of the gods. Hubris comes in many forms, as ancient thinkers like Plato and Aristotle realized.

In later chapters I will examine in detail Huizinga's and Feezell's alternative account of athletics as play, in partial contrast to Weiss's thesis of athletics as the search for bodily (human) excellence. Feezell's account even more than Huizinga's relies heavily on a first-person singular (or phenomenological) perspective. Here I wish to highlight the fact that Weiss's only limited experience of playing athletics leads him to say some odd things.

For example, he says that spectators do not want to participate in athletics (in contrast to the more plausible view that they often *want* to participate but cannot do so, at least not at the highest level); that excellent athletes achieve their status largely through rigorous discipline (in contrast to the more defensible view that excellent athletes sometimes are hard workers and sometimes are just "natural athletes," as is the baseball player Ken Griffey, Jr.); that sprint records should take into account wind enhancement (they do); that success in weight training is measured by how high the weights can be lifted (in contrast to how much weight is lifted or how many reps can be performed); that an incomplete pass in football is the same as a fumble (the two are quite different); that the item attached to the rim on a basketball court is called a "headboard" (it is actually called a "backboard"—headboards are on beds); that spectators stretch *at* the seventh inning of a baseball game (rather than in the middle of the seventh inning); that football players cohere more as a team than baseball players (perhaps Weiss is correct here, but he needs to supply a reason for his view); that one does not score a touchdown in football even if one gets the ball to the goal line (actually, if the ball crosses the plane of the goal line, a touchdown *is* scored); that luck, seen as the overall effect of contingency, plays a bigger role in athletics than in other areas of life (not in my experience, at least); that those who try out for college teams have approximately the same talent level but are distinguished primarily in terms of their level of aggressiveness (in contrast to the more defensible claim that they differ significantly in talent level); that basketball coaches are more inclined to view victory as the primary goal of athletics than football coaches (really?); and so on (Weiss 1969, 14, 17, 106, 123–124, 129, 145, 155, 162–163, 166, 186, 206).

4. WEISS AND PLAY

Despite the defects in Weiss's method of detachment from first-person singular approaches to athletics, there is nonetheless much to be learned from him (cf. Ullian 1973), at least as long as his (tendentious) views are brought into equilibrium with other accounts. Very few athletes retire at the top of their game like the football player Jim Brown. More typical is the athlete who "is preparing himself for defeat, and perhaps humiliation.

His days are numbered, his successes rarely momentous, and his glories short-lived; he works hard and long to prepare himself for what may end in dismal failure. Why?" (Weiss 1969, 18).

This is an interesting question, and Weiss's outsider response to it is nuanced. Granted, he thinks that athletes endure all of these things in order to be excellent. In addition, however, he notes that athletes often *like* to train, that they are satisfied by the rigors of the athletic life in a deep way, that they gain in some way even in defeat, and that athletics is often engaged in for its own sake—it is "autotelic," in his usage (Weiss 1969, 18, 21, 30, 110). In this regard Weiss reminds us of Miller and Spivey, who, it will be remembered, seem to have both affirmed and denied the idea that ancient Greek athletes competed in "sport for sport's sake." And in this regard the usual distance between Weiss, on the one hand, and Huizinga and Feezell, on the other, is lessened. Weiss even goes so far as to say of athletes that "athletics gives them a surplus of joy no matter what they do. Their failures and frustrations merely accentuate the inextinguishable glow that is theirs when they give themselves fully to a life of sport" (Weiss 1969, 22). So the athletics-as-play thesis is not entirely outside of Weiss's ken. But the purpose of such joyful activity is ultimately, he thinks, the pursuit of bodily excellence. This is due to the rather wide gap he usually sees between the playful activities of children and the inability of sound-minded adults to really play (Weiss 1969, 24).

The challenge that Weiss poses to proponents of the play theory of athletics like Huizinga and Feezell is clear:

> Sometimes it is said that we must make men play, but what is then intended is a reference to the necessity that they relax. We want them to stop taking themselves so seriously, and to begin to enjoy something, or themselves, for a time. If we wish them to play as children do, we must help them assume a position they once had in the past. But it is rarely that an adult can, without self-consciousness, retreat far enough back to recover the position where he can really play. And if he is self-conscious, he will not play as children usually do. A man may cast off serious concerns and indulge his fancies, experimenting idly and at random. This will not make him a man at play, but at best merely exhibit him to be at ease or without a care. (Weiss 1969, 69–70)

Casting off serious concerns, yes, but play, no, Weiss seems to be saying. But there is still the problem of trying to explain why nonserious athletics itself is taken so seriously. We should also notice in this quotation the fact that play is a retreat, as was the ancient *gymnasion-palaistra* complex, in contrast to the *agora* and *bouleuterion*, as we have seen Spivey argue.

In any event, on Weiss's account as young boys grow into men they play less and less. If they continue to engage in athletics they largely do so for external reasons. These externalities include the effort to maintain bodily health, the desire to attract women, and especially the drive to be excellent, he thinks. If we are made morally excellent through athletics, rather than merely physically excellent, this does not so much reflect favorably on athletics as it reflects negatively on the rest of the educational system, which should be centered around the moral improvement of the young. As is well known, athletics can also hinder growth in character, as when young athletes are lionized and are encouraged to succumb to hubris (Weiss 1969, 25–28).

Weiss notices how odd it is to call tuition waivers for college athletes "scholarships." Perhaps this locution is acceptable if it serves to sever the connection some make between athletic competition and war. Once again, the excellent athlete is one who both accepts the body and its limitations *and* aggressively tries to improve it, as in the aforementioned Platonic *dynamis*. But this "aggression" is hardly war. Contra Spivey, Weiss views even the aggressive element in athletics as a constructive activity (Weiss 1969, 184–185). Or better, if we stipulatively distinguish, along with James Parry, among assertiveness, aggression, and violence, we can understand Weiss's point better. Assertiveness involves moving freely in an athletic competition and taking advantage of one's game-specific rights. Aggression involves the use of physical force as one asserts oneself in an athletic contest. And violence involves the intent to harm others through one's aggression. Weiss's point seems to be that assertiveness in athletics is a good thing; aggression can be a good thing, depending on the athletic contest in question; and violence should always be avoided in athletics, even in quasi-combat athletic events like boxing, some versions of which could be nonviolent and morally permissible (Parry 2002, 259–263).

Although Weiss consistently underemphasizes natural athletic ability, he is right to suggest that bodily excellence almost always requires some degree of dedication. One is not likely to unite successfully with the body, to become a hylomorph (once again, from the Greek *hyle*—matter—and *morphe*—the structure or form given to matter by mind or soul) in a purely passive way. That is, Weiss's hylomorphism is (at least for men, as we will see) aspirational rather than metaphysical; to become a mindbody is to accomplish something after much effort. To call such dedication "self-sacrifice," however, as Weiss does (*askesis*, or "training," would be better), works against his own observation that athletes often *like* to train. But a mental vector is needed so that one does not become dedicated to an impossible goal, as in planning to play in the NBA when one is over fifty years old and under six feet tall (Weiss 1969, 67).

We have seen that ancient Greek athletic games were often integrally connected to what Weiss calls "the equipped body": the *hoplitodromos* (race in armor) required shield and helmet; the *halma* (long jump) required weights; the discus and javelin throws required a *diskos* and *akon*, respectively; and so on In the contemporary world, too, there is a seemingly endless series of "continuations of self" provided by athletic equipment: bats, skates, horses, rackets, clubs, sticks, gloves, helmets, specialized shoes, and so on.

Ideally an athlete becomes one with the body, a hylomorph. So also the athlete ideally becomes one with the equipment that continues the self. For example, longtime catchers in baseball hardly notice their weighty and (to an outsider) cumbersome equipment, otherwise called "the tools of ignorance." The catcher's mitt *becomes* one's catching hand. Likewise, a polo player *becomes* something of a contemporary centaur. That is, the boundary of the athletic individual often becomes the limit of the athletic equipment (Weiss 1969, chap. 5).

But an athlete is not a puppet or an object. Athletes must decide on a *strategy*, conceived as a general course of action, as well as on more particular *tactics*. In many sports it is typically the coach who is responsible for the former. However, even if a coach decides on strategy, the particular athlete is not, or ought not to be, unreflective. To paraphrase Kant, judgment without skill is empty, skill without judgment is blind. Of course, as Weiss uses the term, childlike "play" does not require judgment if it stands for aimless frolicking without rules. In athletic events that are rule dominated, however, some intellectual element is required.

This Greek need for balance or moderation has implications for an external goal that is often associated with, rather than integral to, athletics: health. Athletes tend to fall short of mental health, or *eudaemonia* in Aristotle's sense of the term, but they nonetheless typically acquire a type of health that is more than an absence of disease. The Anglo-Saxon root of the word "health" is related to wholeness, in this case a bodily wholeness, a certain bodily power to act properly. A convenient summary of Weiss's overall stance can be found in the following:

> An athlete can . . . be treated as offering one step in a progress toward the state of being a full, matured, i.e., a completely healthy, man. Having achieved a bodily excellence, the athlete can go on to try to master the other dimensions of himself, and so eventually become excellent on every side. Occasionally we hear of men who have done this. But for most it is more than enough to achieve the state of being excellent in some more limited area. For the young man there is nothing he is likely to do as well as make himself be an excellent functioning body. And there is hardly a better opportunity for doing this than that provided by contests and games. (Weiss 1969, 99)

Here Weiss comes close to resigning the young athlete merely to the *kalos* half of the more complete Greek ideal of *kalokagathia*, to physical excellence without the intellectual, to *kalos* without *agathos*.

Nonetheless, it is important for the athlete as nascent intellect to understand exactly what is being tested in an athletic event. In a sprint it is speed. However, it is common to see the fastest pitcher on a baseball team be less successful than other pitchers who throw slower. As the cliché has it, there is a difference between being a mere thrower and being a true pitcher. So here speed is an important factor, but not the only, nor necessarily the crucial, factor that is needed. The sprint example is closer to baseball pitching than initially seems to be the case, however. In a sprint there is also the matter of getting out of the blocks, or in the ancient Greek sprints of getting out of the *balbis* (Miller 2004a, 31–46). If speed were the only issue, there should be an acceleration period in sprints similar to that in some auto races so that only speed would be tested (Weiss 1969, 104).

Weiss rightly bemoans the lack of a fixed vocabulary in athletics. For example, in the United States (and in the present book) "sport" is largely used as a synonym for "athletics," whereas in the United Kingdom and elsewhere "athletics" is used mostly for track and field events, as I have noted previously. There is something to be said in favor of the criticism of American usage here. We have seen that "to sport" originally meant to divert or amuse. It does not quite convey the *agon* and desire to win found in the etymological root of "athletics." Likewise, there is also something to be said in favor of *some* sort of distinction between play and athletics, as Weiss emphasizes (perhaps overemphasizes). Children and puppies play, but not us, he thinks. The point seems to be that, although we take athletics seriously, this seriousness is not as weighty as that found in other activities, as in eliminating grinding poverty, worshipping God (if one is a theist), or caring for one's children. Once again, Weiss at least flirts with the athletics-as-play hypothesis, even if ultimately he rejects it.

For some unstated reason, Weiss thinks that Roger Caillois is a more reliable guide to the athletics-as-play hypothesis than Huizinga. (Feezell, by way of contrast, gives equal respect to Huizinga and Caillois.) Caillois sees play as exhibiting the following six characteristics:

1. It is *free*. Weiss is not entirely convinced here, because sometimes children are forced to play, they are deliberately sent outside to play, say, if the parents have work to do inside.

2. It is *separate* from ordinary life. Here Weiss sometimes agrees with Caillois, as in his characterization of at least some athletic contests as autotelic. As Weiss puts the point, "He who wants to be refreshed through play must forget about refreshing himself, and just play" (Weiss 1969, 110, 137). This characterization of athletics as play is complex, however, in that very often athletics is seen as a locus for character development, which is very much part of ordinary life. In this case it is not autotelic, but propaedeutic to what will occur later in real life (Weiss 1969, chap. 9; Caillois 1961).

3. Athletics is also *uncertain* in the sense that the outcome of an athletic event is not known in advance, in contrast to a theatrical performance.

For example, the audience knows that by the end of *Oedipus Rex* the lead character will be blinded, but no one knows for sure who will win the next World Cup in soccer. Weiss agrees with Caillois here.

4. As Caillois sees things, athletics is also *unproductive* regarding economically viable goods. Weiss agrees with Caillois here, too, but Weiss drives a wider wedge than Caillois between play and professional athletics. Even professional athletes almost always *like* to play their games and often retire only when the game is no longer fun (say, if it hurts to play due to injuries or old age). In any event, athletics is unproductive in the sense that one can easily imagine a society that flourishes without athletics (but not one that entirely lacks play, according to Huizinga); one cannot do the same regarding a society without food.

5. Despite the disanalogy to theater in point 3 above, an athletic event is like drama in that it involves a *make-believe* element. Here Weiss agrees with Caillois that the athlete must assume a role. We will see, however, that Huizinga and Feezell are much more explicit and much more insightful on this point than either Weiss or Caillois.

6. Athletic events are *subject to rules*. Again, Weiss agrees with Caillois.

From the above one can see that Weiss agrees with Caillois regarding points 3, 5, and 6 and partially agrees (and hence partially disagrees) with him on points 1, 2, 4. These partial disagreements are enough to make Weiss's view sufficiently different from the athletics-as-play stance as to require a different label: athletics as an avenue to pursue bodily excellence, especially in young men. Consider the following startling assessment on Weiss's part:

> It is when a child plays that it usually is most a child, but a man is normally most a man only when he stops playing and tries to do some justice to his responsibilities. A child is at its best when it plays. A mature man who plays is always less than what a man might be. The young man is in between. It is all right for him to play some of the time because he is not yet able to do more important things; it is not right for him to play all the time for there are other, more useful or noble things he could do. . . . Though the athlete is rarely playful, he often has his moments of innocent exuberance and pleasure; his primary tonality is satisfaction for having done what he ought, and not, as a child, for having done what he wanted to do. (Weiss 1969, 139–141)

It should not surprise us that Weiss's distaste for adult play sounds, especially in the last lines of this quotation, very Kantian.

5. GAMES

Games in general need not involve bodily excellence (e.g., chess), but athletic games in particular do, on the Weissian view. (We might note at this point that "game" comes from the Teutonic *gamen* and involves, like "sport," amusement or delight, but also the idea of a contest according to rules.) Just as there is a danger in overemphasizing play (e.g., by completely reducing life to it), there is also a danger in overemphasizing games (e.g., by seeing *any* intelligible activity as a game, as in the later Wittgenstein). Turning an ankle so as to be unable to play in a "big" game is not to be equated with becoming disabled so as to be unable to earn a living. Life is not a game, as Weiss correctly sees things. (We will see that Feezell partially disagrees.) Hence, when we play games, we should keep in mind their relatively nonserious character and keep the pursuit of victory moderated. Cheating and deliberately attempting to injure an opponent indicate a total misunderstanding of what athletics is all about (Weiss 1969, 149, 151).

One of the reasons why games are taken very seriously is that they are often associated with solemnity, ceremony, even a religious aura, as in the eternal flame at the contemporary Olympics, which in some vague way harkens back to the eternal flame of the Prytaneion at ancient Olympia, sacred to Hestia, the goddess of the hearth (Miller 2004a, 87).

Or again, athletic games are associated not only with solemn affairs, bordering on religion, they are also often associated with nationalism and can carry with them propagandistic baggage. We pay a price, Weiss seems to be saying, in tallying Olympic medals according to country (or according to city-state, as in ancient Greece); we also pay a price in encouraging nationalistic rivalries by playing patriotic anthems before, during, or after each game. Defense of athletics also ought to avoid enthusiastic submission to the mindset of generals, politicians, and business executives (Weiss 1969, 28, 152–157).

Games are often closely tied not only to religion and patriotism, but also to history. Even the solitary golfer, in Weiss's example, is comparing himself to the great figures in the history of the game. In team athletics especially there is a strong sense of being part of something bigger than oneself, of being part of a tradition where records mark the passage of time. Athletics is also in some way larger than life because it is so public. Even if Weiss hyperbolizes when he says that those who excel athletically only in private are possessive of some character defect (many other explanations of public mediocrity are possible), he is nonetheless correct in identifying some of the factors involved in being overly serious about athletics: religion, nationalism, and history (Weiss 1969, 158–171).

A more modest approach to athletics is one where the outcome of games would not be seen as so important that one would argue with officials. The ancient Greek officials at athletic events (*Hellanodikai*), it will be remembered, carried a *rhabdos*, a rod used to physically punish offenders (Miller 2004a, 17). Weiss is no prude, however. He would permit arguing with officials if such behavior were part of the ritual of the game in question, as in the familiar scene of a baseball manager arguing a close play at home plate with the umpire, in contrast to the decorum that is expected on a golf course. Weiss rightly assumes (along with almost all great athletes) that bad calls made by officials will balance out in the long run, or even in the short run, as in an NBA game where one does not have to wait too long for a "makeup" call when a referee makes a mistake (Weiss 1969, 171).

One of the reasons why athletic competition has such a wide appeal is that, at least when individual competitors or teams are evenly matched, the publicity of a game brings out hidden strengths and deficiencies of the athletes that might not have been predictable. Games allow for finer discriminations among athletes that would not be made if we did not take athletic competition so seriously. Athletic competitions are telling examples of the indeterminate becoming determinate (Weiss 1969, 173).

Weiss is walking a fine line here. On the one hand, his overall stance regarding athletics as the pursuit of bodily excellence would seem to lead him to accentuate the desire to win more than Huizinga and Feezell, who defend the athletics-as-play view. On the other hand, Weiss's view that athletics is not as important as other pursuits in life, his view that life is not a game, leads him to deemphasize victory in sport. As an example of the latter tendency in Weiss, he claims that the emotions that are developed in athletics (e.g., the agony involved in a losing *agon*) are not as nuanced or as sensitive as those found in art (Weiss 1969, 175).

Because of his skittishness regarding the desire to win in athletics, Weiss does not want to romanticize ancient Greek athletics, where the drive to win was crucial, even if his own account is heavily Platonic (as we will see) and Aristotelian. For example, we have seen that, unlike the contemporary Olympics, the ancient games at Olympia (in contrast to the chrematitic games) gave no acknowledgment to second- and third-place finishers. Only the winners were rewarded and memorialized. Very often the hegemony of interest in victory in athletics goes together with a tendency to push athletics and war together. Although many athletic contests do, in fact, have a military origin (boxing, martial arts, dressage, relay races), Weiss insists along with Miller that athletics is not war. This is true in part because killing the opponent violates the spirit of games, but such a practice is integral to war (Weiss 1969, 176–185).

Another way to put the point is to say that an athletic event involves a sort of bracketing that is not required in (indeed, it seems to be opposed to) war. That is, participants in war are very much aware of the fact that they are confronted with reality, rather than with something separated from it. Although principles of just war are intended to civilize war and to make it morally permissible, there is nothing like handicapping weaker teams or participants so as to make the fight fair. In the still largely Hobbesian world of international relations, last place finishers are not allowed to choose first in the next draft.

This is ultimately due to the fact that in a game one's opponent is not really an enemy. It is not often noticed that the Latin root meaning of "competition" is to struggle *with* rather than *against*. (Think of two boxers at the end of a long fight congratulating each other.) In war, by contrast, there are real enemies. Regarding the relationship between war and athletic events, respectively, Weiss says the following: "The one is a serious enterprise casting its shadow over the whole of life; the other is a serious enterprise encapsulated by rules which bind and define an isolated domain" (Weiss 1969, 183). But athletics can be used to prepare for war, so those who are interested in preserving the autotelic domain of athletics should be aware of this sort of degeneration. Athletics offers an opportunity to channel aggression in a harmless way. It provides the space to find what we have seen James call "the *moral* equivalent of war," in contrast to Orwell's darker "*war* without the shooting." In Weiss's language, "Sport is not aggression controlled and harmless. It is a constructive activity in which aggression plays a role" (Weiss 1969, 185; James 1984; Orwell 1968, emphasis added). Once again, "competition" refers to struggling *with* another; if it meant struggling *against* another the word would be "antipetition" or "contrapetition."

6. PROFESSIONALISM

Weiss's emphasis on the pursuit of excellence through athletics *should* lead him, it seems, to concentrate on victory in athletics, but he is prevented from doing so by the fact that he ultimately sees athletics as less important than other activities (e.g., art). Likewise, Weiss's emphasis on the pursuit of excellence through athletics *should* lead him, it seems, to defend professional athletics. Not having to earn a living outside of athletics is no doubt conducive to focusing exclusively on athletics so as to better achieve bodily excellence. But Weiss especially admires a literal amateur athlete, one who loves athletics and who plays it, ironically enough, for the sake of playing itself. Professionalism tends to militate against the autotelic character of athletics in that the external good of moneymaking can easily compromise the athletic activity. Every contemporary sports fan has his or her favorite example that illustrates how this has occurred. Nonetheless, Weiss is correct to emphasize that today "the line between amateur and professional is mainly a line between the unpaid members of a privileged class and the paid members of an underprivileged class" (Weiss 1969, 192–193, 198).

Because of professional athletics and highly organized amateur athletics, we have come to think of spectators as essential to athletics, but this is not the case. Spectators (and television viewers), however, certainly make possible large salaries for athletes. And herein lies the apparent reason for Weiss's distaste for professional athletics: although an independent source of income allows the professional to be a better *athlete* (Weiss misleadingly says it makes the professional a better "player," which is not, I think, what he really wants to say), it does not encourage the professional to be a better *person*. In fact, great wealth seems to work to the detriment of character development of persons because, in Platonic and Aristotelian fashion, it encourages *pleonexia*, an insatiable desire for things. Weiss notes that this is indeed an old problem that goes back to the time of the Greeks, as Miller and Spivey have also noticed (Weiss 1969, 204; Segal 1967).

Professional athletes, Weiss correctly notes, are more likely than amateur athletes to be viewed as entertainers. Big-time college athletes are also likely to be viewed in this way. Colleges and universities are diminished by this sort of "professionalization," as they are as well when professional schools within the university acquire hegemony over more academic disciplines. The task is to return to the attitude of a true amateur, a lover of the game or of the academic discipline, even in the midst of the pressures of professionalism: "Professionals and amateurs are different. . . . The one works for money, the other plays as part of an adventure at self-discovery and growth. The one wants to do a workmanlike job that has value for his employers, whereas the other seeks to help to bring about a game well-played. The task of the professional is to please, usually by means of a victory; the task of the amateur is to function excellently in the game. The objective of the one is economic security . . . , but the objective of the other is to become more of a man" (Weiss 1969, 209). Once again, there is an identity in difference between Weiss's athletics-as-pursuit-of-bodily-excellence hypothesis and the athletics-as-play hypothesis of Huizinga and Feezell. That is, we will see that the above quotation is not entirely opposed to what Huizinga and Feezell are trying to say.

7. WOMEN AND ATHLETICS

We have seen that Weiss's "outsider" status frequently enables him to see things about athletics that "insiders" miss. We have also seen that this approach leads to some questionable claims. These defects are especially evident in what he says about women and athletics. Later we will see Feezell challenge the "ageism" in Weiss's claim that it is primarily *young* men who pursue bodily excellence in sport. Here we will focus on the sexist claim that it is young *men* who primarily exhibit such a pursuit. Among the questionable claims are the following: that women fatigue more readily than men (when in point of fact the evidence from marathons and fifty-mile races seems to run in the opposite direction), and that women are more individualistic and are less team-oriented than men (evidence?) (Weiss 1969, 214, 221–222). That is, Weiss's view of women and athletics is largely in a state of disequilibrium with respect to what most other philosophers of athletics want to claim.

Because women, in general, are less muscular than men, there are only a few athletic contests where they can compete meaningfully with men. And these athletic contests tend to be those that privilege grace, as in figure skating or diving. Weiss insists that he does not view women as truncated men. Indeed, he relies on Aristophanes' speech in Plato's *Symposium* in suggesting that men and women share a common desire to be complete. Fewer women than men tend to compete athletically because they are already closer to completeness than men. For Weiss men *ought* to be hylomorphs who have some sort of unity between mind or soul, on the one hand, and body, on the other. But because they tend to be dualists who use mind to dominate their own or others' bodies, they must strive to achieve this unity. Women, by way of partial contrast, are naturally at home with their bodies. Hence, there is a danger that they will lose their femininity, he thinks, if they train and compete like men. This "at homeness" with the body is due to the fact (assuming for the moment that it is such) that women tend to be less concerned with abstract reasoning than men (Weiss 1969, chap. 13).

It does not escape Weiss's notice that the (alleged) differences between men and women that he highlights (or invents) might be due to the pervasive influence of history and culture, rather than nature. But he largely rejects this hypothesis. The tenor of his view is found in the following statement regarding a typical woman: "Her mind functions on behalf of her body in somewhat the way in which a trained athlete's mind functions on behalf of his. A woman, therefore, will typically interest herself in sport only when she sees that it will enable her to polish what she had previously acquired without thought or effort" (Weiss 1969, 218). Because of this felicitous harmony between (or, stronger, unity of) mind and body, women typically "are not subject to the tensions that young men suffer—tensions resulting from the discrepancy in the ways in which their minds and bodies tend to be disposed; the women have already achieved a satisfying integration of mind and body" (Weiss 1969, 220). Therefore, in order to interest women in athletics it might be necessary, he thinks, for women to try temporarily to separate from their bodies only to return to them later. Although Weiss at several points speaks of athletics as autotelic, of athletics as an end in itself, his more usual view is that the *telos* of athletics is to enhance the formation of good habits so as to improve character. Women, he seems to be saying, are less in need of such habit formation because they are less likely than men to be restless, pleonexic, and subject to violent explosion (Weiss 1969, 226–227).

It is easy to criticize Weiss's view of the relationship between women and athletics, but we would be remiss if we did not notice that there is at least a grain of truth in what he says about young male restlessness and explosiveness. A test case: imagine reading in the daily newspaper about a mass murderer who had just killed several local citizens. Is it not the case that we would assume that the murderer was a male? Would we not be shocked to find out that the murderer was a female?

Jane English provides a useful counterweight to Weiss's view such that, by considering her stance, we can see what is defensible and what is indefensible in Weiss. She agrees with Weiss that adopting an attitude of strict nondiscrimination in athletics, where sex is irrelevant, would lead to fewer opportunities for women. That is, if women had to compete with men in many athletic fields (soccer, baseball, football, sprints, swimming, etc.) they would fare poorly and few of them would "make the team." This is especially instructive given Plato's (apparent) support of this view in book 5 of the *Republic* (English 1978; also Postow 2002).

The issue of women's talents in athletics is even more complicated than Weiss realizes, however. In some sports (e.g., on the balance beam and in some other skills in gymnastics) women tend to perform better than men; in other sports they clearly tend to perform worse (e.g., in the blocking skills required of offensive linemen in football, which rely primarily on brute strength); and in some sports women seem to be the equal of men (e.g., in putting skills in golf); and in still others we just do not know very much about women's abilities. This ignorance is perhaps due to historical and cultural factors, which Weiss acknowledges but de-emphasizes, that have led to an attenuated sense of what women's athletic abilities could be. Might it be the case that a woman will one day win a tournament on the PGA tour and not "merely" on the LPGA tour?

In general, however, English agrees with Weiss that there should be equal chances for athletes *as members of* a certain sex. Basic benefits should be available to all such that if a sufficient number of women wish to play football, there should be a women's football league available to them. Hence, like Weiss, English thinks it appropriate that there be competition classes according to age (as in the ancient *paides* games for youth, or as in the contemporary seniors' tour in golf), weight (as in contemporary wrestling or boxing), and sex. Weiss controversially adds race to the list on the assumption that in some athletic skills blacks are naturally superior to whites (Weiss 1969, 238; cf. Mosley 2002; Burfoot 2002). Further, English thinks that those in a lower weight category should be permitted to "move up" to a higher weight class if they wish, but a heavyweight should not be permitted to "go down" in order to easily defeat middleweights. Likewise, women should be permitted to compete with men if they are capable of doing so, but men should not ruin women's athletics by, say, playing in women's softball leagues so as to win the home run title.

Further, English, like Weiss, thinks that new sports should be invented for women, based on precision and grace rather than strength, that would allow them to excel in their own way. In an oblique way English agrees with Weiss that women do a better job of moderating the competitive spirit than men such that there is little danger that they would allow athletic competition to degenerate into violence.

On at least two issues, however, English is quite different from Weiss. First, English leans heavily toward the athletics-as-play hypothesis such that the key thing is to play, if you wish, and to have fun, whereas Weiss concentrates much more on playing *well*, indeed on playing in an *excellent* way. The resource allocation issues that would seem to be entailed by Weiss's view would be disastrous, from English's perspective. Second, Weiss's belief that men are more attuned to abstract thought than women, and hence more predisposed toward dualism, would seem to be anathema to English.

Stripped of its sexist baggage, however, there is room for rapprochement between Weiss's view and the approach taken in English's influential article. The main piece of sexist baggage is, if the mixed metaphor be allowed, the echo of Ares (the god of war) in the Greek cognate *arete*. The dedicated life of the athlete is not essentially connected to violence, however, and it does have the commendable effect of discouraging human beings (not only men) from acting unreflectively on bodily impulse. Ultimate goods are pursued both by the scholar (e.g., truth) and the athlete (e.g., fair and friendly competition). And it would be nice if there were individuals who could pursue excellence in both ways.

The athlete resembles all of us in at least one additional respect: his or her body eventually decays. At least for a while, however, the athlete can unite local matter or a particular body with the meaning of human life itself: by enriching and mediating our neo-Aristotelian understanding of the extent to which human beings can perfect themselves (Weiss 1969, 248).

8. PLATO AND ATHLETICS

In this final section of the chapter I will contend, as promised, that Plato's dialogues exhibit a wide-ranging set of beliefs concerning athletics; Plato did not denigrate athletics as the character Socrates did in the *Parmenides* regarding the alleged forms of hair and mud. Further, I will try to show how evidence from Plato's dialogues amplifies Weiss's view of athletics. It is interesting to note that many colleges (e.g., Michigan State), high schools, and athletic teams have as their nickname the "Spartans." Perhaps Weiss noticed this too. But although Sparta may have cultivated athletics in a way no other state has, athletic education need not be "Spartan." I will organize my remarks around certain themes that are apparently important to both Plato and Weiss.

1. Plato seems to have had in mind a system of athletic *education* that was lifelong. Exercise is most important in childhood, especially to the age of five, in that the body grows at a greater rate here than in the rest of

life. When a body is subjected to a vast increase in bulk without exercise, the results can be disastrous (*Laws* 788D–789A). But the maintenance of that bulk must continue to the end of life (*Republic* 403D), as even Weiss would admit. Bodily exercise, however, need not be a ball and chain to which a human being is slavishly tied. Human beings *like* to move their bodies in that they are active creatures by nature. This is most evident in young boys (a Weissian commonplace), who find it impossible to keep still (*Laws* 653D, 672C, 673D). One might say that a human being (male or female), for Plato, is a *Homo athleticus*.

The task of the educator is to take this natural proclivity to use one's body and harness it so that it is used properly in a Weissian way. In a well-known part of the *Republic* (410B–C) the proper preliminaries for the education of youth are outlined. There are two generic areas: "music" (which develops the soul), and "gymnastics" (which develops the body). Each of these areas covers a much wider range of activities than is signified in the contemporary uses of these terms; hence, I will refer instead to intellectual education and physical or athletic education, respectively.

We should be clear that *all* human education is for the sake of the soul (also see *Protagoras* 326B). A purely athletic education (*Republic* 410B–C, 535D) leads to a condition close to savagery (*agriotetos*). The goal is to advance to more formal studies, as mathematics or even philosophy (*Republic* 521D–E). And these two prefatory studies are ultimately connected with Plato's and Weiss's greater metaphysical concerns. That is, athletic education prepares one to understand the world of becoming in that it presides over the constant growth and decay of the body, while intellectual education ("music") anticipates some of the discoveries to be made in more formal disciplines.

In the *Laws* Plato discusses in a bit more depth what these preliminary studies should be like, although they are no longer intended to culminate in the development of a philosopher-king or philosopher-queen, as was the case in the *Republic*. The initial studies for children in athletic education should, in turn, be of two types: dancing and wrestling (795D–796A). Dancing actually forms a link between athletics and intellectual education in that it is intended to develop dignity in the child. Wrestling is advocated because it fosters physical fitness (contra Spivey). The athletic endeavor should not, on Platonic or Weissian grounds, be for idle vainglory, but should contribute to the overall development of the child.

The proper blending of intellectual education and athletic education also renders the parts of the soul concordant (*Republic* 441E), especially the bodily part that constantly tries to buck the rule of reason, as does the wayward steed in the *Phaedrus*. Unfortunately, this blending is not easy, as Weiss also notices. For one thing, serious intellectual study is much more demanding than serious athletic activity (*Republic* 535B). For example, Socrates' arguments are often more difficult to disentangle oneself from than a wrestler's hold (*Theaetetus* 162B, 169B), as we have seen. Or again, if one thinks physical exercise is difficult, one should see the rigorous gyrations demanded of a dialectician (*Parmenides* 135C). Because of the difficulty of study, and because of the pleasures of the athletic life, some only engage in the labors of the body, at the expense of the soul, and become one sided (*Republic* 535D). This might be seen as foolish at the very least because even if we love bodily exercise, it cannot love in return (*Lysis* 212D). But it should be noted that the opposite extreme is also possible, as Weiss argues. The mathematician who becomes so absorbed in intellectual pursuits that physical exercise is abandoned entirely is also one sided (*Timaeus* 88C; *Protagoras* 326B–C). Remaining true to the popular sophrosynic maxim "Nothing in excess!" Plato along with Weiss advocates a mixed life.

In the myth of Er, Atalanta transmigrates to an athletic life, an intermediate life between the best and worst types (*Republic* 620B). In the *Laws* (743E) Plato arranges the three major objects of human interest in order. The good of bodily health is sandwiched in between the goods of soul and the goods of possession. And in the *Phaedrus* (248) athletics is given an in-between status among many other nobler and baser activities. Weiss would seem to agree with these orderings.

Mind or soul should always have the upper hand; once again, Weiss agrees. Whereas a sound body does not necessarily make a soul good, a sound soul (i.e., a truly intelligent one) *does* make a body the best that is possible (*Republic* 403D). To let oneself get hopelessly out of shape, it seems, shows ignorance of biology, if not of other studies. "Musical" education, through fables, should begin before the physical education of the child in each session to show this priority (*Republic* 376E). The priority here is logical and need not play into the hands of an ontological dualism.

In addition to the above-mentioned benefits of the athletic life, as well as the intrinsic worth of a healthy body, other benefits accrue. Only by being tested in physical trials, Plato seems to think, can one see whether a prospective ruler will be courageous enough to hurdle intellectual trials (*Republic* 504A). Also, the well-trained body is more likely to enable the soul to be well trained or temperate (*Laws* 839E). This is because the more the appetitive part of the soul is trained the more the rational part can be about its proper business. But just as a well-trained body brings benefits, a poorly trained one brings hindrances, as Weiss also notices. For example, although proper physical education leads to a healthy desire for victory, an overemphasis of this desire makes these victories problematic (*Laws* 641B–C). Thus, although Plato would not seem to oppose organized children's athletics on prima facie grounds, he would oppose them if they came to be taken too seriously. And writ large, states that cultivate the body too much lend themselves to faction, just as the overly cultivated body of an individual causes a divided soul (*Laws* 636B; cf. *Symposium* 182C).

2. In addition to shedding light on athletic education, the characters (especially Socrates) in Plato's dialogues also deal insightfully with the relationship between athletics and *sophistry* in ways that are very similar to those advocated by Weiss. The passage that most directly goes to the heart of the matter is in the *Gorgias* (464B–465D). Here we find one of Plato's favorite devices: the four-term analogy. There are four activities that make an individual good. Two deal with the body and two with the soul. One activity in each of these pairs deals with the prevention of illness and one with its cure. The analogy goes as follows:

"gymnastics" : legislation :: medicine : justice

We have seen that "gymnastics" is the activity that, when performed well, leads to health of body. But because bodies are by nature destructible, an activity is needed to repair the body when it is ill or injured; this is medicine. Likewise, if a soul proposes to itself good rules to live by (or if the rulers propose good laws to the state) the soul will be healthy. This law-giving activity is legislation. But because perfect laws seem impossible, justice is required to adjust the injustices that are the results of some laws.

The point to this analogy, however, is that "gymnastics," or the athletic life, and legislation are the primary and far more important activities, to the chagrin of doctors and lawyers. Plato seems to be implying that a society that glorifies doctors and lawyers may well do so because of its inability to properly foster athletics and legislation. Medicine and justice are called into play only when athletics and legislation need help. Admittedly, even in the best of circumstances these activities will need help. Although the athletic life can make the body as healthy as possible, it cannot make it indestructible, as Weiss also notices. And although law can rationally order what is not rational to a degree, complete rationality seems out of the question. One reason for this is the fact that laws deal in generalities and can only encompass particular details with difficulty. This is exemplified by track coaches, who deal with the general rules of training and running, and not with each individual step of the runners (*Statesman* 294D).

In fact, the analogy in the *Gorgias* anticipates the discovery of relative nonbeing in the *Sophist*, or the unlimited factor in the *Philebus*, or the nonrational character of the receptacle in the *Timaeus*. Medicine and justice, in large part, owe their existence to these unintelligible factors built into the world we live in, just as irrational numbers are built into the structure of mathematics. Plato is not quite the overly ambitious rationalist that many make him out to be. But then again, medicine and justice are often propagated because of the failure of a people to make a "stitch in time save nine" by first getting their bodies and souls in the best shape possible through athletics and Weissian wise legislation.

There is another analogy in the *Gorgias*, however. It has the same structure as the previous one, but the four activities offered here are those that flatter the individual by aiming at the pleasant instead of the good. In other words, these activities are inadequate imitations of the previous four activities. This analogy goes as follows:

beautification : sophistry :: cookery : rhetoric

Sophistry, which is a pretender to true philosophic legislation, sways the individual away from rational law by all sorts of inadequate means that would be excoriated by Weiss. Rhetoric makes the same sorts of pretensions regarding justice.

My concern here is with "beautification" and "cookery" (*kommotike* and *opsopoiia*, respectively), which are seen as mischievous, deceitful, ignoble, and irrational (*alogon*) arts (*technen*). Beautification includes all of those devices that deceive one into believing that one has true health, which only the athletic life can produce. This deception can be accomplished through altering shapes and colors, or by smoothing and draping the body with an alien charm. Presumably Plato has in mind here the cosmetics, fashion techniques (as in fancy warm-up suits), and deceptive devices (as in weightlifting for physique rather than for real strength) used to this very day and anathema to Weiss. The charm of these things is alien because it only covers the body like a veneer and can never produce the core of health as can reflective *askesis*. Even a cursory glance at our society reveals a people who are often more interested in *looking* healthy than actually *becoming* so.

Likewise, cookery includes all of those attempts to regulate eating habits and give remedies such that they are always pleasant, instead of aiming at true health, which often demands a medicine that is unpleasant. In the *Gorgias* passage it is noted that those who want to be restored to good health only through pleasant means are like children who want to grow big and strong solely through sugary treats. At times the extent to which the advertising industry today succeeds in this regard with its thoroughly childlike appeals to *adults* is surprising. The key point is reiterated: "gymnastics" and medicine are the true arts of the body (*Gorgias* 517E–518A; *Sophist* 228E–229A). The athletic life, therefore, when properly practiced, is, as Weiss holds, just as much opposed to sophistical devices as is philosophy itself. When practiced improperly, however, it becomes one of the guises for the sophist to hide behind (*Protagoras* 316D).

3. Further, various characters in Plato's dialogues are instructive regarding the character of *athletic events* that are morally appropriate. There

is no indication that Plato would have changed the Athenian law of his day requiring a father to give his son a physical, as well as an intellectual, education (*Crito* 50D). In fact, the state was required to provide facilities where such education could take place. Such facilities included exercise space and warm baths, as well as training grounds for the various athletic events (i.e., a *gymnasion-palaistra* complex). As we have seen, these facilities would be connected to schools. Apparently, more important contests would be held on grounds built on top of the graves of dead leaders of the state, signaling the communal spirit of the games (*Laws* 761C, 804C, 947E; also *Euthydemus* 272E–273A; *Lysis* 204A–206E; *Protagoras* 312B, 335E; *Charmides* 153A; *Euthyphro* 2A; *Symposium* 223D).

One suspects that Plato witnessed some athletic games at which fans yelled "Kill the ump!" in that explicit instructions are given to appoint overseers so that the games would not be disorderly (*Republic* 424B). This preservation of good sportsmanship is advised for both the participants and the spectators in that displays of anger reduce the stature of athletic events (*Laws* 935B), as Weiss also emphasizes. In the *Laws* the status of the overseers of athletic events is seen as so important that it becomes an elected position (*Laws* 764C, 765C, 828C, 832D, 835A).

Honest referees should be found, however difficult this may be (*Laws* 949A). (A recent NBA scandal regarding gambling and the corruption of ice skating officials a few years ago at the Olympics make us realize that this difficulty is still with us.) These officials would have to be multitalented, as they would have to officiate everything from human events to horse races (*Laws* 764D). The implication seems to be that if an honest referee can be found, the particularities of the various athletic events can be learned easily enough. But the ideal condition is one in which there is an objective standard for determining a winner, thereby minimizing the referee's responsibility, as we have seen Miller emphasize, and as in Weiss's chapter "The Standardization of Sport." Events that foster the attempt to pander to the crowd should be avoided (*Laws* 658A).

A history of athletics can be detected in the dialogues. It began with the Cretans and eventually reached the Lacedaemonians, including the Spartans. Athletes first competed wearing clothes, but eventually they saw the convenience of nudity (*Republic* 452C). The first nude competitions created quite a stir; this will occur again when women become athletes and compete in the nude, as they should (*Republic* 452A–C; *Laws* 772A, 804E, 813B–E). In the *Republic* (456A–457A) the thesis is advanced that there are three types of women just as there are three types of men. Therefore, there should be philosopher-queens as well as female soldier-athletes and female carpenters. Despite his historical distance from us, Plato often seems more egalitarian and more in line with contemporary feminist views (e.g., English's stance) than Weiss.

The importance of athletics in Plato's view of the just society is made clear both in discussions of really important topics, like sophistry, and in more trivial matters, such as rewarding the state's best with the prime seats at athletic events (*Laws* 881B). Further, hindering an athlete from competing, so as to help an opposing athlete or state, is a heinous crime (*Laws* 955A). In the *Laws* (832D–834D), where much of Plato's thought on athletics is evidenced, a very specific program of how athletic events should be organized can be found. Several ancient Greek and Weissian commonplaces are also to be found. For example, those who exhibit excellence by winning should be rewarded, yet vainglory is to be denounced. As before, the attainment of moderation (*sophrosyne*) is admittedly difficult, but this is precisely the ideal that Plato and Weiss defend. The program of events is not too different from that of the Olympic Games, although archery is added in the "Platonic Games" and the *pankration* is quite understandably modified, if not eliminated (*Laws* 795B, 834A; also *Greater Hippias* 295C; *Lesser Hippias* 373C–373E; *Charmides* 159C; *Protagoras* 335E; *Meno* 94C; *Theaetetus* 162B, 169B; *Euthydemus* 277D; *Sophist* 232E).

We have seen that there were objections to boxing and the *pankration* in Plato's day; his view seems to have been that the purpose of these athletic contests should not be to seriously harm other people (*Gorgias* 456D). If others are harmed, the trainer is not to be blamed, although the rules of the athletic contest may have to be altered to assure safety (*Gorgias* 460C). As with wrestling, the references to boxing in Plato's dialogues are not few in number (e.g., *Laws* 795B, 796A, 830E; *Republic* 422B). And fencing and archery are also frequently cited (for fencing see *Euthydemus* 271D, 273C–E; *Laches* 178A, 179E, 182A, 183C; *Laws* 795B,

813E, 833E; for archery see *Lesser Hippias* 375A; *Laws* 625D, 804C, 805A, 813D, 833B, 834D).

I mentioned above that the program of athletic events in Plato's dialogues is not too different from that at the Olympic Games. However, the notion that women should participate, and participate in the nude, was novel. Plato seems to acknowledge the legitimacy of ancient athletics; or at least he does not have them polemicized in the dialogues. Like Weiss he seems to want to perfect them, to make them conducive to the best in human beings. But a tension that we saw in Weiss is found in Plato's dialogues as well. On the one hand, the cultivation of excellence in athletics would seem to require professionalization in the sense that the athlete cannot make a living outside of athletics if his or her training schedule is too time consuming. On the other, Plato along with Weiss denigrates those who cultivate athletics in a one-sided way (*Laws* 807C–E) in that this one-sidedness seems to be at odds with *sophrosyne*.

Perhaps this tension can be resolved by an appeal to the full sweep of Plato's career. The program outlined in the *Republic* is literally a utopian one that exists "no place." That is, one cannot be a true intellectual and an Olympic champion at the same time. Plato seems to realize this more clearly in the *Laws*, where he is more practical. Although an overdevelopment of athletics is still seen as detrimental to the development of character, we may have to pay this price, but only with respect to the most gifted Olympic aspirants. Such license should not be granted, it seems, to their less able imitators.

We have seen that there is evidence that Plato himself was a wrestler at the Isthmian Games, and he apparently attended at least one Olympic Games (*Seventh Letter* 350B). If Socrates did not attend any Olympic Games, he at least came into contact with some who did (*Lesser Hippias* 363C, 364A, 368B). Further, the Olympic Games find their way into several of Plato's writings (*Apology* 36E; *Republic* 465D, 466A, 583B; *Phaedrus* 227B; *Laws* 807C, 822B, 839E, 950E; *Second Letter* 310D). But it should always be remembered that there are many things in life more important than even an Olympic victory (*Laws* 729D), which is precisely Weiss's point as well.

4. Because of critiques of athletics by scholars like Spivey, it is

worthwhile to return to the topic of *athletics and the military* as it relates to Plato and Weiss.

Generally speaking, Plato along with Weiss thinks that athletics plays a necessary, but not sufficient, part in the development of a well-rounded person. If one has not received physical training as a child, one can still obtain it in later years, even if this means a bit of pain at the beginning of training (*Laws* 646D). This offers some consolation to the middle-aged and out-of-shape, who are largely left out of Weiss's view of athletics. But everyone, it seems, can find some athletic contest appropriate to his or her body, although it might mean overcoming the embarrassment of playing ball like a child (*Thirteenth Letter* 363D). (We have seen that Weiss is somewhat reticent regarding the ability of adults to really play.) For the more hardy, in addition to athletic endeavors already mentioned, perhaps a strenuous tug-of-war will do (*Theaetetus* 181A) in preparation for a wrestling match. Or perhaps something that would develop ambidexterity, as archery (*Laws* 794E–795D).

Plato seems to have been aware, however, of the pitfalls of being a "weekend athlete." If one gets sick or injured, one should not deceive oneself or one's trainer about one's physical condition (*Republic* 389C). One way to avoid injury and sickness is to always allow an ample length of training time before exercising strenuously, especially for more rigorous events like boxing (*Laws* 830A–C). All of this suggests that Plato himself, in contrast to Weiss, was as well versed in the particularities of athletics as in those of the arts and mathematics.

Training of the body need not be divorced from other concerns in life. We have noted that one can cultivate both the arts and physical training through certain types of dancing, for example (*Laws* 673A). But just as Plato notices the interpenetration of bodily training and art, so also he sees the confluence of bodily training and the military. There is, however, no identification of athletic training and the military; hence, the view advanced here is closer to Weiss's and Miller's stance than to Spivey's. Nonetheless, the fact that some athletic activities can serve the purpose of preparing the populace for military service, or can help to develop a frame of mind that is violent in character, indicates that Spivey's thesis will not go away easily and must be taken seriously in the effort to achieve some sort of reflective equilibrium. Plato even seems to be willing to live with the possibility of *deaths* that would result from war games (*Laws* 813D, 830D–831A, 865A).

At no point, however, does Plato give evidence of having been persuaded entirely by a Spartan (or Cretan) attitude toward the relationship between athletics and war. To cite a famous example, the guardians of the *Republic* are themselves athletes who need to have their athletic abilities governed by a rational agent for them to be of value both to themselves and to the state. They need to watch not only their diet, but also their desire for wealth and their desire to have a bodily regimen dominate their lives (*Republic* 403E, 404A, 422B, 543B). In fact, the whole orientation of Plato's attempt to do philosophy works against the Spartan (or Cretan) mode of looking at athletics. Unfortunately, from a Platonic or Weissian point of view, this aspect of ancient Greek culture has often gone unnoticed. I am shocked to learn that Crawfordsville High School in Indiana adopted as its nickname the "Athenians."

5. Although athletics is admittedly one of Plato's secondary interests, his concern for it does appear throughout the dialogues from the *Apology* to the *Laws*, with many of the other dialogues in between included, especially the *Republic*. This seems to indicate both that athletics is interesting in its own right and that it helps illuminate topics that are of highest concern to Plato: sophism, the need for moderation, and so on. In this regard Plato helps us to better appreciate Weiss's contemporary defense of the athletics as search for bodily excellence hypothesis.

Elizabeth Spelman is correct to note that very often in Plato's dialogues one can find indictments of the body, leading to a sort of "somatophobia" that is troublesome from a feminist point of view (Spelman 1995). However, it should be remembered that the denigration of the body, found especially in the *Phaedo* at a time when the body was of little concern to the character Socrates, does not typify all of Plato's thought. It is also important to note that an area of contemporary society that receives so much attention (perhaps Plato along with Weiss would say that it receives too much attention) can perhaps be understood better when viewed from afar, from the perspective of an extremely wise person from a quite different culture and a distant historical epoch.

Plato seems to have realized that athletics has a unique potential to act as an impetus to true *civic pride*. Having lived much of my life in Philadelphia, I can testify that the Phillies, Eagles, 76ers, and Flyers have done more to unite the citizenry of that city (for good or for ill) than brotherly love. In book 2 of the *Republic* and book 3 of the *Laws* Plato makes it clear that what *should* be the glue that keeps society closely knit is a reasoned awareness of the justice inherent in a community of human beings living together, and of the benefits derived from that community. Perhaps this brief viewing of athletics in our society through Platonic and Weissian eyes can intimate to us where we have succeeded in this regard and where we have gone wrong.

Huizinga and the *Homo ludens* Hypothesis

1. INTRODUCTION

In this chapter I will try to accomplish five things. First, I will show that Huizinga's *Homo ludens* hypothesis is rooted in a Platonic concept of play that is seldom noticed by those thinkers who (mistakenly) assume that the ancient Greek *agon* was incompatible with the concept of play. Second, I will then discuss the *Homo ludens* hypothesis itself, indicating what it entails and what it does not entail. Third, I will also consider the *Homo ludens* hypothesis as it relates to the concepts of language, culture, and knowledge. Fourth, I will then return to the topic of violence, specifically to the relationship between play and violence, to show how Huizinga's approach to the topic adds something crucial to our understanding of this relationship not found in Weiss. Finally, I will examine the view of human reality *sub specie ludi*, a view that will further illuminate Weiss's stance and will prepare the way for a consideration of Feezell's stance in the following chapter. That is, this chapter will provide a useful bridge between those dedicated to Weiss and Feezell in the effort to reach some sort of reticulation regarding the various options in contemporary philosophy of athletics that are rooted in ancient thought.

2. PLATO AND PLAY

It would be a mistake to think, as a result of the previous chapter, that the view of athletics found in Plato's dialogues is a matter for simple classification. It is to Huizinga's credit that he highlights a view that is somewhat different from the athletics-as-pursuit-of-bodily-excellence hypothesis; there is, in addition, the athletics-as-play hypothesis. It will be the purpose of this section to examine Plato's place within this latter hypothesis.

Huizinga relies on a key passage from the *Laws* (803) where "the Athenian" (presumably Plato's spokesperson in this dialogue) compares what we today would call a plan of life with the work of a shipwright. The shipwright begins the work by laying down the keel and then builds the outline of the ship. The "keel" and "outline" (*schemata*) of the best life (*bion arista*) are provided by the advice that life should not be taken too seriously, from the ancient Greek word for seriousness, *spoudaios* (Huizinga 1955, 18–19).

Granted, from a pragmatic point of view we have to be earnest about our lives (which the Athenian thinks is a pity). The wisest course, however, is to show this earnestness in a suitable way, by saving our seriousness for serious things rather than for trivialities, but also by realizing that the only *really* serious reality is God. That is, we should treat even our "serious" matters playfully, from the Greek word for play, *paidia*.

Two further points are made in this passage that are crucial in the effort to understand Huizinga's view. The Athenian makes it clear that (1) human beings are God's playthings, and (2) this is the best thing about us! (see Hyland 1977). Although interpenetration with a concern for excellence is possible, in that we are enjoined to make our play as perfect as possible, one cannot help but think that something distinctive is going on here. In fact, it seems that in this part of the *Laws* there is an inversion of both ancient Greek and contemporary common sense, which suggests that work is for the sake of play. The view advanced here, by contrast, is that play is either autotelic or for the greater glory of God: *ad majoram Dei gloriam* (the anachronistic Jesuit motto seems appropriate here).

Huizinga even speaks of Platonic play as "consecrated." His purpose is not to trivialize religious practice or other sacred realities. Rather, it is to consider carefully the implications of the idea that life should be lived as play, whether the play be that of children leaping or that of adults performing political or religious rituals (also see *Laws* 653, 796). Huizinga is well aware of the fact that the ancient Greeks at least nominally distinguished between *paidia* (play) and *agon* (contest), but there is an "essential oneness" between the two, he thinks, as is evidenced when Plato has even armed dances played (Huizinga 1955, 27, 37, 48).

Or again, in the *Sophist* (222D) we are alerted to the playful aspects of legal activity, an activity that Plato seems to take quite seriously in the later dialogues. One can turn a bad cause into a good one, it seems, by playing with words. Further, the ancient Greek myths at one point may have been taken with deadly seriousness; eventually they were abandoned altogether. But in between they were taken with a grain of salt; they were still seen as important, but only with qualification. This half-joking element is evidenced frequently in Plato's dialogues (e.g., *Sophist* 268D; *Symposium* 223D; *Philebus* 50B). Like Shakespeare, Plato seems to have seen the whole of human life as a blend of tragedy and comedy (Huizinga 1955, 87, 130, 143, 145).

One consequence of Huizinga's treatment of the *Homo ludens* theme in Plato's dialogues is that we are led to see Plato's treatment of the sophists in a new light. The familiar charge that the picture of the sophists Plato gives us is a caricature or parody might be somewhat blunted if playfulness itself had a more honorific place in Plato's philosophy than is normally assumed to be the case. Admittedly Plato always seems to be opposed to what we today call Machiavellian manipulation of words for reasons of personal or political aggrandizement. But dialectic itself appears to be a noble game, even if it is nonetheless more serious than eristic. The first ancient Greek dialogues, which were the models Plato had before him, were farces (*mimos*), offshoots of comedy. There is clearly a *scherzo* quality to many scenes in Plato's dialogues, the most obvious of which is Alcibiades' drunken entrance at the end of the *Symposium*. And Plato was well aware of the charge (*Gorgias* 484C) that philosophy itself was sophomoric and hence comic when practiced into adulthood (Huizinga 1955, 147–151).

The hallmark of Huizinga's view is a certain fusion of play and seriousness that leads (in Feezell especially) to an intellectually rich view of athletics. He is well aware of the criticism he will receive to the effect that the Greek word for play, *paidia*, is etymologically associated with the word for what is childish. Hence, some contemporary thinkers (e.g., Keating 1964) tend to think of "child's play" as a redundancy. But there were other ancient Greek words that helped to solve this problem: *agon* (contest), *scholazein* (to take one's leisure), *diagoge* (to pass the time), and so on. All of these retain in some sense the spirit of play, even if the ancient Greeks did not have one generic word that captured this spirit. It will be remembered that Spivey hinted at the idea that for the ancient Greek freeman the task in life was to figure out how to spend one's leisure time (*schole*), how to enjoy autotelic activity without the assumption that it had to produce something else (Huizinga 1955, 159–160).

The ancient Greek freeman did not have to work for a living; hence, it was easier for him to have the option to idle well ("scholazein dynasthai kalos"—Aristotle, *Politics* 1337B) than it would have been if one were female or a slave. But now there are many more "freemen" (including many women) than there were in antiquity; hence; ancient insights regarding the joy of playful activity might be given new efficacy. If life is lived as play, it is crucial to decipher what the noblest playful games are, in contrast to those that dehumanize us. As Huizinga puts the Platonic point, and once again religiously, "The human mind can only disengage itself from the magic circle of play by turning towards the ultimate" (Huizinga 1955, 161–162, 211–212; also see *Phaedrus* 276D, 277E).

Highlighting the *Homo ludens* dimensions in Plato's dialogues is nonetheless compatible with the serious attention paid by Plato, Aristotle, the Stoics, and others in ancient Greece to the life of virtue. For example, one reason to keep the spirit of play alive in athletics is that athletics is fraught with contingency, as in the possibility that at any moment an athlete could suffer a career-ending injury. To paraphrase Martha Nussbaum, our bodies as well as goodness are fragile. Aristotle, in particular, emphasized the fact that we cannot shield ourselves entirely from contingency and that at times bad luck can have a major effect on how our lives will go. The Stoics, however, and at times Plato, indicate that the good life involves shielding ourselves from contingency to the extent that this is possible. On either approach, however, a certain lightheartedness is required in order to avoid being swept away by events outside of one's control. Nonetheless, Feezell and William Stephens make a convincing case for how even Stoicism (once a simplistic version of Stoicism is rejected) is compatible with *caring*, in some fashion, for athletic victory (Nussbaum 1986; Fry 2004; Bergmann Drewe 2001; Simon 2007; Feezell and Stephens 2004).

As before, seeing athletics as play is compatible with serious philosophical pursuits. For example, Plato's *Republic* can be seen as a test of hypotheses regarding justice that is strongly analogous to an athletic test. The best view of justice should carry off the prizes (612D—*niketeria*), on this view (Reid 2007). Further, justice is both good in itself and good for its effects (358A); so also with athletic contests. To eliminate the "in itself" dimension of athletic contests (i.e., to see them as strictly instrumental goods) is to eliminate the crucial play element in them (Midgley 1974, 240).

3. THE *HOMO LUDENS* HYPOTHESIS

Huizinga's own view is meant to provide an alternative to two other views of human nature that have been dominant since the Enlightenment: the human being as *Homo sapiens* (the human knower) and *Homo faber* (the human maker). *Homo ludens* (the human player), he thinks, is a more powerful explanatory device than either of these, as we will see. A common misunderstanding of Huizinga's view is fostered by a mistake in the subtitle of his book that was forced on him by others: he is concerned not with the play element *in* culture, but with the play element *of* culture. The former compartmentalizes and trivializes play in ways that are inaccurate, he thinks (Huizinga 1955, foreword).

In other words, play is *really* basic in the sense that it colors most of life and goes all the way back in evolutionary history to the nonhuman animals, as when dogs gambol or kittens toss about a round object. Here at the start we see the controversial nature of Huizinga's view. The tendency on the part of many scholars is to see play as something else, say, as preparation for the serious business of predation in the cases of dogs and cats, or as the contemporary opiate of the people, as in some Marxist critics of athletics. But the intensity and absorption of play activity, Huizinga argues, resists natural or social scientific efforts at reductionism (Huizinga 1955, 1–2).

Neither nonhuman animals nor human beings mechanically go about their activities; hence, it makes sense for Huizinga both to sidestep theories that rely primarily on mechanism and to recur to ancient Greek authors, among others, who had a richer view of human nature than that defended by mechanists or reductionists. In effect, play *begins* where biology and psychology leave off. Suppose we ask, Why do birds sing after mating season is over and when territory is not threatened? (Mating and defense of territory are the two primary reasons for birdsong on the mechanical grounds defended by animal behaviorists.) The most parsimonious response is to say that they *like* to sing and *desire* to avoid boredom. They play at singing (Hartshorne 1973; Dombrowski 2004, chap. 4). Likewise, Huizinga tries to take human play as the player, rather than as an outside observer, takes it (Huizinga 1955, 4).

It was quite common in the seventeenth century to see all the world as a stage, all of us as players, and everything else *sub specie ludi*. This is a variation on the biblical theme of the vanity of all things. Hence, there are clear historical roots that lie beneath Huizinga's quite original contribution. This contribution lies primarily in an opposition to the current tendency to see play as the opposite of seriousness. Soccer, to take an obvious example, is played and watched with "profound seriousness." That is, folly and comedy are not to be identified with play (Huizinga 1955, 5–6).

There are three crucial characteristics of play that enable Huizinga to offer something that at least approaches an essential, rather than merely stipulative, definition of play. First, contra Weiss, play is *free* activity. Without broaching the issue of free will versus determinism, Huizinga sees play as free in the sense that it is a liberating, enjoyable activity done at leisure. Second, related to the freedom of play is the fact that it is *separated* from "ordinary" or "real" life. Hence, play involves a "pretending quality." It is, in a sense, disinterested, an interlude of sorts or an intermezzo, even if the play in question becomes a habitual part of life in general. Third, and related to the separateness of play, it is *limited* in time and place. It begins and ends, on the one hand, and it occurs in some specific place, on the other. Indeed, sometimes this specific place is special, even sacred, as has often been noted regarding the baseball diamond. It is such separateness and limitedness when considered together that makes play a fecund ground for memory and for the dating of the passage of time, as in the ancient Olympic Games, as we have seen (Huizinga 1955, 7–10).

As Bernard Suits has emphasized (Suits 1967), play governed by rules occurs in games. These games, on Huizinga's view, are worlds within the world with their own limited perfections. Indeed, Huizinga notes the proliferation of aesthetic terms used in everyday discourse to describe these playful games: tension, poise, balance, harmony, contrast, monotony, variation, resolution, and, of course, beauty itself. The point can clearly be overemphasized, as when an aesthetically pleasing, albeit missed, shot in basketball is valued more than an aesthetically displeasing one that nonetheless goes through the hoop. But the tense, dramatic character of play is readily apparent, especially in the sort of competitive play that occurs in athletic contests (Huizinga 1955, 10–11).

The tendency might be to constantly analyze athletics in ethical terms, wherein the cheater receives the greatest opprobrium. But if we see athletics as play, aesthetic analysis is just as important, in which case it is not the cheater but the spoilsport who is the nadir. This is because the cheater at least pretends to take seriously the "magic circle" of play in the effort to gain unfair advantage within it, whereas the spoilsport shatters the play world itself. He or she just refuses to keep alive the play spirit. The magic of play, notes Huizinga, can even create a sense of community wherein, once the play is over, the players are "apart together." This is evidenced when a game is re-created many years later in memory; every athletic team member who is not a spoilsport understands the point here (Huizinga 1955, 12).

Huizinga sums up his position with the following definition of play: "We might call it a free activity standing quite consciously outside 'ordinary' life as being 'not serious,' but at the same time absorbing the player intensely and utterly. It is an activity connected with no material interest, and no profit can be gained by it. It proceeds within its own proper boundaries of time and space according to fixed rules and in an orderly manner. It promotes the formation of social groupings which tend to surround themselves with secrecy and to stress their difference from the common world by disguise or other means" (Huizinga 1955, 13). The "disguise" Huizinga has in mind might mean nothing other than the fact that the players wear uniforms, or at least distinctive athletic gear. More on "profit" later.

I should make it clear that I am not the least bit skittish about Huizinga's agreement with a Platonized version of religious belief or with the place of play within such belief. Obviously this is not the place to defend a position regarding the epistemology of religious belief (see Dombrowski 2005; 2006). But it is appropriate to notice that when Huizinga talks of play being *outside* of ordinary reality, he sometimes means *above* ordinary reality in a higher realm, a "mystical" or ecstatic (literally *ek stasis*, "outside of one's normal place") realm, in his usage. This stance rests foursquare on Plato's view in the *Laws* (803–804).

Further, the sacred space of play is not a place where the sacred is merely imitated; rather, it is concretely enacted or performed. To use the appropriate ancient Greek terms, play is not mimetic (from *mimesis*, or "imitation"), but methexic (from *methexis*, or "participation"). It is common today to hear about athletic rituals; it is not so common to find scholars taking these rituals as seriously, as religiously, as Huizinga. We have seen that ritual play is continuous with nonhuman animal play and with child's play, but it is also continuous at the other end with hieratic ritual typically found in religion (Huizinga 1955, 14–17). No doubt the connection Huizinga makes between play and holiness will strike some contemporary readers as hyperbolic or wrongheaded. As before, his point is not to defile religion, but to exalt play. "The sportsman . . . plays with all the fervour of a man enraptured, but he [*sic*] still knows that he is playing" (Huizinga 1955, 18).

Perhaps Huizinga's view here can be made more plausible by considering a thinker whom he cites in an offhand way: Romano Guardini, who was an influential theologian in the early decades of the twentieth century. Guardini notes that earnest, supposedly serious people often have problems with both athletic play *and* religious liturgy. The allegation is that athletic play and liturgy are alike in being childish and aimless and full of superfluous pageantry, and they are trifling and theatrical for no reason.

Guardini's response is to say that there are many worthwhile areas in life that are not purposeful in the way that a bridge or a machine is. Theatrical performances themselves are not purposeful in this way; neither are examples of athletic play or religious liturgy. But to say that athletic play or liturgy or a theatrical performance (in everyday English, and quite understandably, a play) do not have a purpose is not to say that these lack meaning. To put the point positively, to say that these things lack purpose is to say that they are ends in themselves, and ends in themselves can be quite meaningful. That is, by escaping from the hegemony of purposiveness one may train the *psyche* to develop more playful, artistic, and religious sensibility (Huizinga 1955, 19; Guardini 1997, 61–71).

Along with Plato, Huizinga thinks that there is no clear distinction between clearing out a time and space for play and doing so for a sacred purpose. To be precise, "frivolity and ecstasy are the twin poles between which play moves" (Huizinga 1955, 21). The ludic function is evident in both play and religious belief in that in both there is activity outside of (or above) the necessities of everyday life that must be taken seriously; and in both there is always an element of ritualized make-believe (Huizinga 1955, 22–27; Rahner 1965; also see Thomas Aquinas's [1972] *Summa Theologiae* IIaIIae, q. 168, a. 2).

4. LANGUAGE AND CULTURE

Huizinga thinks that the *Homo ludens* hypothesis is enhanced by evidence of play words from languages around the world and from different historical eras. This evidence is in large measure what gives him confidence that his definition of play is anything but stipulative. For example, ancient Greek has no less than three words for play, in general. (1) *Paidia*, which we have seen to be etymologically related to childishness, nonetheless denotes all kinds of play, including the highest and most sacred, as in Plato's *Laws*. *Paizein* (to play) and *paigma* or *paignion* (a toy) bring out the obvious lightheartedness and joy associated with all of the cognates of *paidia*. (2) But it should not escape our notice that another word for play, *aduro* or *adurma*, stands for the strictly trifling or the nugatory. That is, there is more weightiness to *paidia* than initially meets the eye. It is tempting to arrange *aduro* at one end of a continuum of play with *paidia* in the middle. (3) At the other end of the continuum of play would be *agon*. We have seen that this last word nonetheless has a ludic character that is not as explicit or obvious as that in *aduro* or *paidia*, but it is definitely there (Huizinga 1955, 28–31).

Huizinga's stance is rescued from the charge of Eurocentrism when the Sanskrit *kritati* is compared to the ancient Greek *paidia* (also the Japanese *asobi*, the Arabic *la'iba*, the Hebrew *sahaq*, and the Germanic *Spiel*), when the Chinese *cheng* is compared to *agon*, and when the Blackfoot *koani/kachtsi* is compared to the *paidia/agon* tension. But he is especially interested in the fact that the Latin *ludus* (and its cognates) is a generic term that seems to cover all of the Greek types of play that lack an umbrella term to unify them; hence the title of his book. Further, in the Romance languages *ludus* is replaced with *jocus* (and its cognates).

Kurt Riezler captures Huizinga's intent when he argues that in the evolutionary transition from worms (which presumably play at ultra-minimal levels) to cats to human beings, there is a progressive escape from dependence and an opening up to a world of voluntary rhythms, sounds, words, movements, games, works of art, and religious beliefs. Art and athletics, he thinks in a Huizinga-like way, are not *merely* play, but they are types of liberating play nonetheless. A human being (albeit an exceptional one) can even write a play like *Merchant of Venice*, which highlights the importance of play in its interpenetration with the serious, as Riezler illustrates: "In the *Merchant of Venice* the relation itself between play and seriousness is the core of the work. Hence its difficulties. In most performances the tragedy of Shylock is put to the fore as the center of the work framed by a playworld of love, fun, music, and sweetness. Such performances can hardly be convincing. If the relation is reversed the performance convinces—a world of play and love put to the fore against the background of a world in which Shylocks hate and suffer" (Riezler 1941, 515). Play is not "mere" play in that it is in dialectical tension with the serious, with what Riezler calls our "ultimate horizon." That is, this serious ultimate horizon provides the background for play, rather than the other way around.

Another admirer of Huizinga's work, Drew Hyland, alerts us to the fact that competitive play can serve the serious function of enabling us to acquire Socratic self-knowledge. Very few activities in life make us aware of our limitations as quickly and as decisively as athletic competition. Likewise regarding the intimate hylomorphic relationship between mind and body (Hyland 1984; 1990, 84–86, 99).

As is well known, Kant was fond of speaking of "the play of ideas," "the play of imagination," and "the whole dialectical play of cosmological ideas." Given the wide range of "play" or its equivalents in other languages, it makes sense in English and other languages to speak of athletic contests, theatrical presentations, and musical performances as examples of play. Hence, we should not accept without qualification the contrast between the Greek *paidia* and *spoude* (play and seriousness, respectively). A better way to relate these terms is to see the serious not so much as contrasting with play but as *heavy* play. The Latin words *serius* and especially *gravitas* are helpful in bringing out this weighty metaphor. A game of checkers with a child is "light," but not necessarily because it is play. That is, "play can very well include seriousness" (Huizinga 1955, 45), as we have seen Riezler argue as well.

I think that it would be a misunderstanding of Huizinga, however, to think that he is saying that human beings evolve into players. Human culture is played from the very beginning, he thinks. No doubt this play element is pushed into the background when the passion to win an athletic contest seems to obliterate levity altogether. Stranger things have happened. This levity is not, however, to be equated with the idea that there is nothing at stake in an *agon*. Granted, there is usually not a material result that is at stake like the material results of ordinary life (unless, say, one is an owner of a sports team or if one gambles on sporting events). But there is something at stake: one's own well-being, the satisfaction (or lack thereof) of having played well (or poorly) and fairly (or unfairly). Hence, it is conceivable (although not likely, according to Huizinga) that even well-paid athletes may be playing their games. The Greek athlete, on Huizinga's interpretation, melts together in a moral crucible several quite different phenomena: exercise, struggle, contest, suffering, endurance, and indeed joyful play. Serious play is thus a complicated matter that is typically trivialized in popular explanations (Huizinga 1955, 46–51).

As an expert not only on the concept of play, but also on the waning of the Middle Ages, Huizinga's unique scholarly talents enable him to see that the origins of the life insurance industry were ludic in character: investors in Genoa and Antwerp played betting games regarding who would live and who would die. Hence, he thinks that Tacitus was at fault for being astonished at the seriousness with which members of ancient Germanic tribes tossed their dice. The fault lay in the erroneous assumption that the serious could be neatly sequestered from the ludic. Tacitus's object of interest (and ours, I am urging in the present book) should have been "'play'—serious play, fateful and fatal play, bloody play, sacred play, but nonetheless that playing which, in archaic society, raises the individual or the collective personality to a higher power" (Huizinga 1955, 53, 57, 61; 1996).

The play *of* culture (in contrast to the play *in* it) is thus, in a way, compatible with the aretic view of Weiss, even if it is in some obvious ways different from it. Indeed, the ancient Greek *arete* is etymologically related to *aristos*, "the best," "the most excellent." Interpenetration, rather than separation, of the agonic and the virtuous is to be expected. Aristotle, for example, speaks of virtue as a prize (*Nicomachean Ethics* 1123D), and in Latin the word for virtue, *virtus*, is derived from the idea of (athletic) virility. It must be admitted that scholars debate the extent to which Burckhardt thought that there was something specifically Greek about the *agon*, but Huizinga resists this parochialism. The fact that play antedates the ancient Greeks, indeed the fact that it antedates humanity, at the very least forces upon us a more expansive perspective. Bragging rituals of all sorts from all around the world, as detailed by various anthropologists, should also encourage us to use a wide-angle lens (Huizinga 1955, 63–75; Burckhardt 1999).

To this very day a courtroom is, as it was in ancient Greece, a *hieros cyclos*, a sacred circle for the reenactment of an *agon*. The judge's gown, like the distinctive jersey of a referee at an athletic contest, indicates the partially make-believe character of the event. Justice (*dike*), whatever else it involves, includes a weighing of evidence and the process of deliberation, which are not unrelated to the athletic labors of the ancient heroes. *Urteil* in German captures this, in that the word refers to both judgment and ordeal. A trial is a test of sorts, an attempt to see whose rhetorical (rather than bodily) dexterity will win the day. As with the origins of life insurance, in several parts of the world trials are accompanied by wagering on the winner. A *litigium* in Latin (the root for our word "litigation") is therefore in many ways continuous with other (including athletic) sorts of *agon* (Huizinga 1955, chap. 4).

5. PLAY AND VIOLENCE

It will be worth our while to see how the *Homo ludens* hypothesis illuminates the relationship between athletics and violence in ways not found in Weiss. Previously we have seen the fruitfulness of conceiving of a continuum of play from mere frolic, at one end, to violent play that borders on war, at the other. The competitive play that is found in athletic contests is between these two extremes. Further, along with James Parry we have seen the fruitfulness of stipulating three different definitions: *assertiveness* involves moving freely in an athletic competition and taking advantage of one's game-specific rights, *aggression* involves the use of physical force as one asserts oneself in an athletic contest, and *violence* involves the intent to harm others through one's aggression (Parry 2002). And along with Weiss we should agree that assertiveness in athletics is a good thing; aggression can be a good thing, depending on the athletic contest in question; and violence should always be avoided in athletics, even in quasi-combat sports like boxing, some versions of which can be nonviolent and morally permissible, say, if headgear is worn and a premium is placed on precision rather than knockouts (Lewandowski 2007).

Joan Hundley may be correct, however, in claiming that one reason for *excessive* aggression and violence in contemporary sport is the overemphasis on the pursuit of excellence, which can be deflected into an overemphasis on winning or on winning at any cost. In turn, she quite plausibly thinks that this overemphasis is built on a patriarchal foundation, even if the particular manifestation of this overemphasis in contemporary societies is also due to other factors. In any event, her view is more compatible with Huizinga's view of athletics as play than with Weiss's view (Hundley 2002). These other factors may very well include the widely accepted (and, I think, dangerous) assumptions that "gamesmanship" and "trash talking" to opponents, on the one hand, and "intentional" fouls, on the other, are morally permissible. These factors often fan the flames of small disputes on the playing field to the point where a major conflagration is the result (Dixon 2002; 2007; Fraleigh 1988). This is "the dark side of competition," to use Stanley Eitzen's phrase (Eitzen 2002; also see Kretchmar 1995).

When Huizinga describes war as a type of (violent) play, he is not necessarily trying to condone it. Rather, he is noting the historical prevalence of calling war a game that is played by rules, which, like athletic rules, are sometimes broken. Although some scholars might be scandalized by the fact that (dogs and) some human beings fight "for fun," Huizinga thinks that it is not the play element that is especially bothersome in war, but its absence. It is in twentieth-century "total war" that the last vestige of the play element is extinguished: there is no chivalric honor, no adherence to rules against killing innocents, indeed no acknowledgment of the fact that there are innocents, and so on. The glory of war, *if* there is such, would lie in fighting fairly (Walzer 2000; Dombrowski 1991, 2002).

Huizinga's stance here is nuanced and worthy of serious consideration. We should not forget that *Homo ludens* was originally published in 1944: "As soon as one member or more of a community of States virtually denies the binding character of international law . . . not only does the last vestige of the immemorial play-spirit vanish but with it any claim to civilization at all. Society then sinks down to the level of the barbaric, and original violence retakes its ancient rights. The inference from all this is that in the absence of the play-spirit civilization is impossible" (Huizinga 1955, 101). Although Huizinga is understandably reticent to agree to John Ruskin's thesis regarding war as the fountainhead of human virtue in general, he does welcome "martial athletics" (e.g., Japanese Bushido) into the sphere of civilized life. Indeed, it was his work on the waning of the Middle Ages that initially led him to the *Homo ludens* hypothesis: chivalric orders and tournaments, and the banners and crests that accompany any noble game, have a residual meaning even today (Huizinga 1955, 102–104).

The recent publication of Roland Barthes's *What Is Sport?* however, is indicative of the fact that the thesis that athletics and war are closely connected will not be going away any time in the near future. Although superior to the unreflective violence of nonhuman animals, human violence in athletic competition is, Barthes thinks, sometimes murderous. Nonetheless, even Barthes admits (along with Spivey and other defenders of a bellicose view of athletics) that athletic competition is often paradoxically engaged in *with* others in a spirit of generosity and with a shared sense of place, say, if the competitors are members of the same nation, city, or even neighborhood. It is perhaps this paradox that makes athletic competition so appealing, to the point where the spectacle of athletic events, where athletes try to determine who is best, now provides the dramatic backdrop for culture once provided in ancient Greece by theater (Barthes 2007, 9, 25, 30, 37, 47, 63).

6. PLAY AND KNOWLEDGE

Archaic cultures, in general, and ancient Greek culture, in particular, were agonistic in structure. But this structure need not promote war more than it promotes knowledge. As in the Chinese yin and yang, in Heraclitus strife is the parent of all things. Athletic doing and daring are admirable, but so is knowledge in the face of adversity. Riddle-solving competitions, for example, were well known all over the ancient world. These contests provided the fertile soil for the growth of philosophy itself. People took riddles seriously because often their very lives were at stake in the solution to them (as was Oedipus's when he was confronted with the riddle of the sphinx). Eventually the effort to "catch" an interlocutor found its apotheosis in Socrates, who threw down intellectual challenges with ease (Huizinga 1955, chap. 6).

Poetry, on Huizinga's view, had its roots in bragging matches (themselves agonic) that very often had as their subject matter some mythic *agon*. It will be remembered that it was not easy for ancient Athenians to distinguish among three practitioners of *agon*: the competitive poet, the

sophistical lawyer, and the philosophical dialectician. Philosophy department meetings even today often degenerate into wisdom matches punc-
tuated by strophe and antistrophe. It is appropriate here to point out one
of Huizinga's definitions of play so as to see both its pliability and to provide the background against which to understand athletic contests: "Let
us enumerate once more the characteristics we deemed proper to play. It
is an activity which proceeds within certain limits of time and space, in a
visible order, according to rules freely accepted, and outside the sphere of
necessity or material utility. The play-mood is one of rapture and enthusiasm, and is sacred or festive in accordance with the occasion. A feeling
of exaltation and tension accompanies the action, mirth and relaxation
follow" (Huizinga 1955, 132). Even agonistic play is sacred and festive
and potentially ecstatic.

One of the reasons why such disparate activities as philosophizing,
reciting poetry, and engaging in athletic competition are rooted in play is
that they all involve a mixed attitude of belief and unbelief. When Saint
Francis of Assisi mythopoetically referred to Poverty as his bride, we suspect that he took such a personification with a grain of salt. Or again,
Hildegard of Bingen's personified Virtues hover in an in-between world
that has fancy and conviction as its termini. Analogous personification
occurs with the theriomorphic names of sports teams: Bears, Seahawks,
Rams, and so on. What children and the preliterate may take almost literally, we take with several grains of salt, albeit somewhat seriously. A half
joke is nonetheless quite a distance from the full-fledged make-believe.
Attendees at a dramatic performance share with sports fans a certain sort
of psychic tension between the serious and the nonserious, an agonic and
tragicomic tension (Huizinga 1955, chap. 7).

The ancient sophist was explicit in his effort to defeat his rivals in a
public contest, indeed in an exhibition (*epideixis*). It is not surprising that
Protagoras was compared to an athletic victor (*Euthydemus* 303A) and
that Gorgias was aware of the fact that his activity was a game (*paignion*).
We have also seen that our word "school" grew out of the ancient word
for leisure (*schole*). The ancient Greeks often spent their leisure dealing
with a particular problem (*problema*), literally something that one put before oneself as a defense or that one put before others as a challenge. The

claim that philosophy is a noble game is compatible with the idea that it grew out of less noble (not exactly ignoble) games like riddle solving and sophistic play (Huizinga 1955, 146–149).

One of the reasons why reading Plato, in particular, is extremely interesting is that we still do not know which passages contain a joke (*griphos*) wherein Plato is pulling our legs, as Richard Rorty has noted (Rorty 1979, 369; Dombrowski 1990). Aristotle explicitly refers to the dialogue form as an offshoot of farces (*mimos*) or other comedy (*Poetics* 1447B). Huizinga's thumbnail sketch of ancient philosophy, when interpreted ludically, nonetheless contains subtle distinctions among the types of play involved:

> We can sketch the successive stages of philosophy roughly as follows: it starts in the remote past from the sacred riddle-game, which is at one and the same time ritual and festival entertainment. On the religious side it gives rise to the profound philosophy and theosophy of the Upanishads, to the intuitive flashes of the pre-Socratics; on the play side it produces the sophist. The two sides are not absolutely distinct. Plato raises philosophy, as the search for truth, to heights which he alone could reach, but always in that aerial form which was and is philosophy's proper element. Simultaneously it develops at a lower level into sophistical quackery and intellectual smartness. The agonistic factor in Greece was so strong that it allowed rhetoric to expand at the cost of pure philosophy, which was put in the shade by sophistication parading as the culture of the common man. Gorgias was typical of this deterioration of culture; he turned away from true philosophy to waste his spirit in the praise and misuse of glittering words and false wit. After Aristotle the level of philosophic thinking sank. (Huizinga 1955, 151)

Later Huizinga indicates that a return to an exalted level of philosophic thinking occurred in the High Middle Ages with the scholastic method of disputation, which was agonistic, polemical, and ludic (Huizinga 1955, 154–157).

7. THE VIEW *SUB SPECIE LUDI*

In the medieval period that Huizinga knew so well, it was common to imagine a view of human affairs *sub specie aeternitatis*: from the perspective of eternity. In our postmodern era there is often an antipathy to metanarratives such that, rather than imagining a divine perspective on human affairs, there are multiple, and often conflicting, views from the perspective(s) of everywhere. In between these two extremes is Huizinga's abductive project of trying to explain as much of human affairs as possible *sub specie ludi*: from the perspective of the ludic.

For example, how should we account for the fact that in English, German, Russian, Arabic, and other languages, musical instruments are *played*? Mere coincidence? A more parsimonious and illuminating response is in terms of the *Homo ludens* hypothesis. In fact, it is very easy in our world today to largely lose the sense of play, but music as much as athletics helps us to regain this sense. In the case of music, this seems to be due to the fact that it elicits in us the deepest emotional experiences. The tension between the nonserious and the serious in music is evidenced, at one end, by the fact that historically music was viewed as divertissement in that musicians were hired on a par with jugglers and tumblers (even Haydn received daily orders from the prince), and, at the other end, by the fact that competition has very often accompanied the deep values with which music is concerned, as in the vocal *agon* depicted in Wagner's *Mastersingers of Nuremberg* (Huizinga 1955, 158, 162–164, 187–188).

From the perspective of the philosophy of athletics it is important to note that the art form that exhibits the purest type of play is dance. This is because there is not play *in* dance; rather, the exuberance of movement of limbs in dance just *is* a type of play: "Dancing is a particular and particularly perfect form of playing" (Huizinga 1955, 165). There is a strong analogy here with the exuberant movement of limbs in athletic activity. The plastic arts are also playful, but the exuberance involved is mediated through paint or clay, and so on. This point can be overemphasized, however, as when it is considered that the ancient Greek word for a celebration is also the word for a statue: *agalma*. Once again, it would be a mistake to ignore the fact that artistic play is often agonic: "The desire to challenge a rival to perform some difficult, seemingly impossible feat of artistic skill lies deep in the origins of civilization" (Huizinga 1955, 169, 172). This point is made readily apparent in the rivalries among the greatest practitioners of the plastic arts in the Italian Renaissance (Vasari 1957).

A useful summary of Huizinga's view is found in the following:

> It has not been difficult to show that a certain play-factor was extremely active all through the cultural process and that it produces many of the fundamental forms of social life. The spirit of playful competition is, as a social impulse, older than culture itself and pervades all life like a veritable ferment. Ritual grew up in sacred play; poetry was born in play and nourished on play; music and dancing were pure play. Wisdom and philosophy found expression in words and forms derived from religious contests. The rules of warfare, the conventions of noble living were built up on play-patterns. We have to conclude, therefore, that civilization is, in its earliest phases, played. It does not come from play like a babe detaching itself from the womb: it arises in and as play, and never leaves it. (Huizinga 1955, 173)

The fact that Huizinga emphasizes the play spirit in the earliest phases of civilization, especially the play spirit in ancient Greece and Rome, leads one to wonder if his *Homo ludens* thesis is part of a greater romantic project. It will be remembered that earlier in the book I tried to distance myself from those (e.g., de Coubertin) who take the utterances from antiquity as a sort of oracular *Ursprache*.

Huizinga's stance regarding romanticism is nuanced, however. On the one hand, romanticism might be seen as opposed to the ludic in its glorification of (supposedly) persecuted artists and heroes with their brooding, gloomy, melancholic, tearful seriousness (see Caputo 1997). On the other hand, the exact opposite seems to be closer to the truth. By reverting to ancient ideals, romantic thinkers open up an "ideal space for thought" that "is itself a play process." That is, their appropriation of the Greeks for the purpose of understanding and critiquing contemporary culture is itself only half-serious: "This precarious balance between seriousness and pretence is an unmistakable and integral part of culture as such, and . . . the play-factor lies at the heart" (Huizinga 1955, 189–191).

I should make it clear that by "romanticism" I have the following template in mind, the details of which can be filled in quite differently depending on the romantic thinker in question: in the "beginning" everything made sense or existed in a paradisial state; then degeneration or a "fall" took place; the goal is to return to the primal source wherein meaning can be restored; this mode of return requires a reorientation of thinking and feeling that itself requires a certain *askesis*, a rigorous training of the mind and will (Blackburn 2000).

Stated in these terms, Huizinga is only partially a romantic theorist. And I am even less so. My own view of the Greek ideals that are the foci of the present book (*arete, sophrosyne, dynamis, askesis, paidia,* and *kalokagathia*) is not that they constitute a primal paradise of ideas with which to examine athletics. Rather, they provide a conceptually interesting standard against which we can judge our own ideals and practices and in terms of which we can better understand the very best work in contemporary philosophy of athletics. As before, to some extent we have improved upon the ancient Greeks, and in other areas we have fallen dreadfully behind them. That is, my own methodology relies only partially on the aforementioned romantic template; my own method is that of reflective equilibrium that involves many different factors, only some of which overlap with romantic concerns.

Huizinga thinks that a combination of factors from the time of the eighteenth century until the present (overestimation of the economic by both capitalists and Marxists, the industrial revolution, the hegemony of instrumental rationality, etc.) has led to a sort of banality: culture is often no longer "played." The conceptual situation is complex. On the one hand, "sport and athletics" have increased in scope; indeed they have "conquered" both national and international imaginations, he thinks. On the other hand, this conquest is ironically often part of the degeneration of the play spirit. The fact that Huizinga distinguishes between sport and athletics does not necessarily mean that he endorses Keating's thesis that sport remains closer to the play spirit than competitive athletics (Huizinga 1955, 195–196).

It is largely Feezell's task to use Huizinga's theory of play in an analysis of contemporary athletics. But before we get to Feezell we should be clear regarding how difficult this project is if, as Huizinga contends, contemporary athletics has largely lost the play spirit. Even before the forces that were degenerative of play developed in the eighteenth and nineteenth centuries, there was the deemphasis of the body in Christianity (in partial contrast to Miller's and Spivey's views), whether Catholic, Orthodox, or Protestant. But despite the "severe intellectuality" of the Renaissance humanists, the Reformation, and the Counter-Reformation, games and bodily exercises endured until the eighteenth century.

In Huizinga's stipulative use of terms, the transition from "athletics," as traditionally practiced, to "sports," in the sense of organized team activities, can be described as follows:

> The basic forms of sportive competition are, of course, constant through the ages. In some the trial of strength and speed is the whole essence of the contest, as in running and skating matches, chariot and horse races, weight-lifting, swimming, diving, marksmanship, etc. Though human beings have indulged in such activities since the dawn of time, these only take on the character of organized games to a very slight degree. Yet nobody, bearing in mind the agonistic principle which animates them, would hesitate to call them games in the sense of play—which, as we have seen, can be very serious indeed. There are, however, other forms of contest which develop of their own accord into "sports." These are the ball-games. What we are concerned with here is the transition from occasional amusement to the system of organized clubs and matches. . . . The great ball-games in particular require the existence of permanent teams, and herein lies the starting-point of modern sport. (Huizinga 1955, 196)

Although some of Huizinga's examples are odd (how is diving a test of either strength or speed? marksmanship?), his general point is well taken. As is well known, the practice of village versus village competition in team games (Huizinga's "sports") started in nineteenth-century England as a result of the structure of social life in that time and place.

The absence of obligatory military training supported the occasion for, and the need for, physical exercises. Clearly the rise of factory towns and the desire of industrial leaders to keep the peace were also major factors. England became the cradle of modern athletic competition in the commons found in every English village. Rules for athletic competition became more rigorous and uniform. Athletic activity was taken much more seriously that it had been taken since the time of the ancient Greeks. Questions arise: Can contemporary athletes preserve (or recapture) the ideals of ancient Greece (*arete, sophrosyne, dynamis, askesis, kalokagathia,* and—especially for Huizinga—*paidia*)? Should such a preservation (or recapture) occur? Might it also be the case that the athlete represents not only philosophic ideals, but mythic ones as well (whether Herculean, Promethean, or Narcissistic)? (Lenk 1985). The following chapter will be especially interested in responding to these questions.

Huizinga is less optimistic than Feezell in his responses to these questions. He is less sanguine than Feezell at the very least for the following reasons:

> Now with the increasing systematization and regimentation of sport, something of the pure play-quality is inevitably lost. We see this very clearly in the official distinction between amateurs and professionals. . . . It means that the play-group marks out those for whom playing is no longer play. . . . The spirit of the professional is no longer the true play-spirit; it is lacking in spontaneity and carelessness. This affects the amateur too, who begins to suffer from an inferiority complex. Between them they push sport further and further away from the play-sphere proper until it becomes a thing *sui generis*; neither play nor earnest. (Huizinga 1955, 197)

A consequence of this attenuation of, or utter loss of, the play-spirit is that athletics is removed from the heart of civilization. This consequence is counterintuitive because of the ubiquity of contemporary athletics:

> In modern social life sport occupies a place alongside and apart from the cultural process. The great competitions in archaic cultures had always formed part of the sacred festivals and were indispensable as health and happiness-bringing activities. This ritual tie has now been completely severed; sport has become profane, "unholy" in every way and has no organic connection with the structure of society. . . . Neither the Olympiads nor the organized sports of American Universities nor the loudly trumpeted international contests have, in the smallest degree, raised sport to the level of a culture-creating activity. However important it may be for the players or spectators, it remains sterile. The old play-factor has undergone almost complete atrophy. This view will probably run counter to the popular feeling of today, according to which sport is the apotheosis of the play-element in our civilization. Nevertheless popular feeling is wrong. By way of emphasizing the fatal shift towards over-seriousness. (Huizinga 1955, 197–198)

Huizinga's cut-and-thrust challenge (to use a fencing metaphor) is clear and deep.

The distance between Huizinga and Feezell, however, is far less than that between Huizinga and Weiss. The loss of the play spirit is due to nothing other than the loss of a childlike attitude that endures into adulthood (which Weiss thinks is almost impossible): "Really to play, a man must play like a child. . . . If not, the virtue has gone out of the game" (Huizinga 1955, 199). Here Huizinga's romanticism is most apparent. We are reminded of Wordsworth's claims that "The Child is father of the Man," that "Heaven lies about us in our infancy," and that the child is the "best Philosopher" (Wordsworth 1981, "Intimations of Immortality from Recollections of Early Childhood"). It would be a mistake, however, to confuse youthful play with its distant cousin: puerilism (Huizinga 1955, 205–206). The latter phenomenon, a blend of adolescence and barbarism or sensationalism, is unfortunately alive and well in contemporary athletics, as in celebratory posturing after a touchdown in football and slam dunk contests among basketball players.

It is to Huizinga's credit that he avoids dogmatism at all costs. That is, he is well aware of the possible criticism his position will receive:

> The attempt to assess the play-content in the confusion of modern life is bound to lead us to contradictory conclusions. In the case of sport we have an activity nominally known as play but raised to such a pitch of technical organization and scientific thoroughness that the real play-spirit is threatened with extinction. Over against this tendency to over-seriousness, however, there are other phenomena pointing in the opposite direction. Certain activities whose whole *raison d'etre* lies in the field of material interest, and which had nothing of play about them in their initial stages, develop what we can only call play-forms as a secondary characteristic. Sport and athletics showed us play stiffening into seriousness but still being felt as play; now we come to serious business degenerating into play but still being called serious. The two phenomena are linked by the strong agonistic habit which still holds sway, though in other forms than before. (Huizinga 1955, 199)

There is a certain flexibility here that will permit rapprochement with Feezell and to a lesser extent with Weiss. All three thinkers, however, are firmly committed to a sense of decency and fair play in athletics.

There is much at stake here. Loss of a sense of decency and fair play is either a cause of, or perhaps an accompanying sign of, the decline of civilization. When we remember that Huizinga's book was written in the late 1930s, and first published in 1944, we can appreciate why he thinks that a society characterized by runaway puerilism is one "rapidly goose-stepping into helotry" (Huizinga 1955, 206). Far better to develop a different kind of power than that to which Huizinga obliquely refers, the "power" that comes from losing gracefully and with self-command in a fair *agon*. Because civilization cannot exist without a certain play element, civilized people demand fair play. Not to do so would be to take competitive games too seriously.

This chapter will end as it began, with an appeal to Plato's apparent view in the *Laws* (685, 803–804) that God alone is worthy of supreme seriousness and that our best feature is that we are able to live our lives as (semidivine) ludic players (Huizinga 1955, 206–213).

Feezell, Moderation, and Irony

1. INTRODUCTION

In the present chapter I will have the pleasure of examining Huizinga's most perceptive commentator regarding the implications of the *Homo ludens* hypothesis for athletics, in particular: Randolph Feezell. As I read the latter, he is primarily a thinker who is working hard to understand the implications not only of Huizinga's *Homo ludens* hypothesis, but also of Aristotle's concept of *sophrosyne*, or "moderation." This explication and defense of moderation in athletics has (understandable) consequences for how we should come to terms with the virtue of sportsmanship, but also (and counterintuitively) for how we should understand the absurdity of *athletics*. However, as we will see, I am not like Feezell in thinking that *life* is absurd.

2. ARISTOTELIAN MODERATION

We have seen that the athletics-as-play view is very much compatible with the presence of "competition." We have also seen that this word comes from the Latin *competitionem*, which points to two parties striving for the same object in a match meant to determine the relative excellence (n.b.) of the two parties. Literally the word is a compound of *petere* and *com*: to strive with, rather than against. Or better, it means to ask with (e.g., whose athletic performance is better?), rather than against. One needs a competitive partner for there to be an athletic contest at all.

Further, competitive play involves a childlike element that is not to be equated with the puerile (from the Latin *puerilis*, for the child*ish* play of adolescents that is either barbaric or sensationalistic or both).

In order to understand the athletics-as-play view found in Feezell, some sort of appeal to Aristotelian moderation is required in that athletics, in general, and the athletic virtue of sportsmanship, in particular, are means between two extremes (which are vices). Aristotle himself saw play (*paidia*—accent on the last syllable), the childlike (*paidia*—accent on the next-to-last syllable), and education (*paideia*) as not only etymologically, but also conceptually related. They involve a sort of lightheartedness that includes wit or a sense of irony. In contrast to this virtuous mean is the presence in some individuals of that which is *agrios*: the boorish or the rude, as ironically exemplified by those who are uncultivated, despite the fact that they might work in the fields. We have seen that a cognate of this word was used by Plato to refer to savagery (*Republic* 410B–D). A related word at this overly serious (and hence vicious) end of the spectrum is that which is *skleros*: dry, hard, rough, and stiff. At the other end of the spectrum is a different vicious activity that is insufficiently serious, as exhibited by the person who is *bomolochos*, or "a buffoon" (e.g., *Nicomachean Ethics* IV.8). It is against this background that Feezell tries to apply the *Homo ludens* hypothesis to athletics, in particular (also see Gaffney 2006).

3 · SPORTSMANSHIP

Feezell's Aristotelian moderation is readily apparent in his treatment of the virtue of sportsmanship, which may very well be *the* most important virtue of an athlete and which deserves a place along with courage, justice as fairness, and the other major virtues. One of the reasons why sportsmanship is a key virtue for citizens in general, and not merely for committed athletes, is that vast numbers of people in contemporary societies come of age morally and are first treated as moral agents at the very time when they are on youth athletic teams. That is, development of the virtue of sportsmanship often goes hand in glove with the development of virtue in general. Or the lack thereof (Feezell 2004a, 83–84).

The most obvious cases of bad sportsmanship are those provided by cheaters, such as hockey or football coaches who instruct their players to deliberately hurt the opposing team's best scorer or quarterback, respectively. Cheaters intentionally break the rules of the game (in this case, the rule against deliberately trying to injure); hence, they engage in a violation of a quasi-contractual relationship. Although it is undeniable that there are elements of athletics that are illuminated by social contract theory, and hence must be brought into equilibrium with other legitimate philosophical approaches to athletics, there are also elements that are best illuminated by virtue ethics: we suspect that the above mentioned coaches are not good people. Less obvious examples of bad sportsmanship often require knowledge of a specific sort of athletic contest: a baseball pitcher who deliberately throws a pitch at the batter's head, rather than "under his chin," as the cliché has it; a volleyball player who refuses to engage in handshaking with opponents after a match; a college football coach who runs up the score on an opponent long after the outcome of the game has been settled; and so on. (Feezell 2004a, 84–85).

One plausible way of dealing with the phenomenon of bad sportsmanship is to appeal to Keating's influential 1964 article, which was later revised in 1978. Keating's fundamental distinction between sport and athletics (which we have seen to be largely based on etymological grounds) supports the idea that the attitudes and behaviors appropriate for playful, sporting activities are "quite different from the norms and responses appropriate for participation in the deadly serious world of competitive athletics" (Feezell 2004a, 85). It is no accident, on this view, that we speak in everyday English of a "bad sport" but not of a "bad athlete." If I understand Feezell correctly, he is bothered by Keating's thesis primarily because, by exorcising the play element from athletics, Keating has, in effect, given the athlete a carte blanche to do almost anything possible to win. For example, note Feezell's use of the word "deadly" in the above quotation. Because Feezell thinks of athletics as a (Huizinga-like) type of competitive play, we *should* have a locution like "bad athlete" as well as that of "bad sport."

Keating makes us aware of the fact that it is by no means obvious that sportsmanship points toward a mean between taking athletics too seriously and not taking it seriously enough. On his view, sportsmanship only applies when we are "playing," as he uses the term, and it is not at all relevant as a mean or otherwise when we are competing for victory.

As I mentioned in the introduction, I was once convinced by Keating's view, but as a result of Feezell's argumentation I have been pulled to a region halfway between Keating and Feezell. If sportsmanship is a key virtue, we need to determine what a sport is. Philosophers in general have been humbled by Wittgenstein, Popper, and others in that it no longer seems possible to offer airtight essential definitions, at least not when we are dealing with controversial concepts like "sport" and "athletics." But it also seems premature to resign ourselves to a pushy nominalism here, wherein "sport" and "athletics" are merely what *we* say they are, whoever "we" may be. That is, we are pulled by both Keating's and Feezell's legitimate concerns, and our definition of "sportsmanship" will suffer and be placed in disequilibrium if both of these considerations are not acknowledged.

There is admittedly a certain experiential pull to Keating's distinction between the spirit of moderation and generosity that characterizes playful sport and the intense competitiveness in athletics that has victory as its *telos*, as was the case in ancient Greece as well. What reflective person who watched the 2006 World Cup final game and its aftermath did not at some point notice the lack of moderation, the lack of generosity, and the lack of playfulness on the part of the "players," fans, and commentators? The verbal taunts, the headbutt, and the endless commentary that followed are exactly what Keating would have expected.

Feezell would presumably agree with the above characterization of the events surrounding the 2006 World Cup final game, but on the grounds of his theory he would not, along with Keating, view these events with equanimity. Something has gone wrong, he thinks, when the play element is lost, even in a big-financial-stakes, international, high-profile athletic event. In this respect Feezell is even more committed to the *Homo ludens* hypothesis than Huizinga in that the latter thought that athletic events *started* in play, but that by the nineteenth century organized team competitions had practically eliminated the play element. Huizinga thereby unwittingly lends support to Keating's fundamental distinction. For Keating (and presumably for Huizinga when analyzing contemporary organized athletics), the prime virtue of the player (i.e., sportsmanship) is radically different from the prime virtue of the athlete (i.e., pursuit not of Weissian excellence, but of victory). Or again, as G. J. Warnock puts it, in a competitive situation things have a tendency to go bad unless there are rigorous moral or legal restraints in place (Warnock 1971; Feezell 2004a, 86).

There is a poem by Wordsworth ("Surprised by Joy") where the narrator turns to speak to his recently deceased daughter, forgetting that she is dead. In this case, it is her absence that is the biggest presence in the room. Likewise regarding the World Cup example mentioned above. It would be odd to hear someone bemoan the loss of a sense of play in war, even though there are rules of war in international law and "war games," as Huizinga notes. We do not really expect war to be played. But Huizinga and Feezell *do* bemoan the loss of a sense of play in contemporary athletics because, presumably, we expect it to be there like the recently dead daughter in the Wordsworth poem. What we really notice is not the taunts and the headbutt, but the *lack* of moderation and the *absence* of play, which, as Feezell rightly holds, *should be* there. Viewers of these events (except for the most maniacal fans, the hooligans) *experience* that something is amiss. In this regard, Feezell thinks, phenomenology trumps Keating-like etymology.

Consider Keating's and Feezell's examples provided by two different high school basketball coaches: Smith and Jones. The former views athletic competition as little short of war. For this coach athletics is either "real life" or necessary preparation for it. By way of contrast, Jones, although he encourages athletes to be competitive and to become as skilled as possible, nonetheless is cognizant of the fact that the athletic competition in question is a rule-governed activity for the purpose of producing an intrinsically satisfying activity: in this example, the "magical" world of basketball (Feezell 2004a, 87–88; also Arnold 2002; Simon 2002).

We can easily understand Keating's radical distinction between these two coaches and his realization that the pressure to win makes Smith's approach at least possible, if not probable: Smith might get fired if a winning season is not produced. But we can also easily understand Feezell's claim that we ought not to take Smith's response to the pressures of coaching as normative. Indeed, we especially admire Jones's view of the opponent as a friendly competitor (once again, literally one whom we strive *with*) rather than as an enemy; and of the seriousness of competition as being moderated by the idea that basketball is "just a game." As Feezell puts the point, "Smith has an impoverished view of sport, an impoverished experience of sport, and it is just such views and attitudes that tend to generate unsportsmanlike behavior in sport" (Feezell 2004a, 88).

In short, Keating underestimates the extent to which play can be extended into competitive athletics by making the player (or the good sport) and the athlete mutually exclusive. Whether or not Feezell overestimates such extension is a matter for debate. Feezell even sees the play spirit at work in high-stakes professional athletic events that others (including Huizinga) view rather cynically. At the very least we should assert that an Ernie Banks–like "Let's play two!" joy is at least possible (if not probable) even when athletes and fans are (or at least are viewed as) commodities.

It is easier for Feezell to make his case with respect to pickup players and weekend athletes of all sorts. These athletes continue to compete well past their prime because they love the games they play. And they love the games they play both because of the exuberance of demanding physical activity and because of the dramatic tension found in the unity of each game they play, whether in tennis, racquetball, or golf. Of course the internal logic of athletic competition requires that one seek victory (e.g., one knows that a volleyball game is over when one side gets to twenty-five points), but the player knows that it is easy to misplace seriousness or to overemphasize it. The reflective athlete realizes that by being a good sport "such an attitude toward the pursuit of victory acts as an inner negation of his original seriousness and produces moderation" (Feezell 2004a, 89).

Herein lies Feezell's insightful extension of Aristotelian moderation into the region of athletics. His approach involves a "both . . . and" feature that enables us to see our way around the Keating-generated "either . . . or" impasse. The good sport "is simultaneously player and athlete. His purpose is to win the contest *and* to experience the playful and aesthetic delights of the experience" (Feezell 2004a, 89). There is no contradiction in being competitive *and* playful and in viewing one's opponent as a competitor *and* a friend.

These matters are especially important in games where there are no referees to adjudicate disputes, as in competitive tennis matches discussed by both Keating and Feezell where there are no line judges and, hence, the participants have to make their own calls. If the spirit of play is not robust, these games can easily dissolve when one of the competitors just walks off the court in disgust or if the game ends with one of the parties getting a gun and threatening violence to the other. I should reply to the charge of hyperbole here by noting that I have actually seen this happen in a pickup (yet serious, indeed overly serious!) basketball game.

Thankfully, athletic competition without paid referees flourishes because usually there *is* a robust sense of play. As before, Feezell (along with Schmitz 1979; and Pieper 1979) is more Huizingian than Huizinga: athletics grows out of play *and still receives* its central values from play, values that are never completely lost or dead (in contrast to the daughter in the Wordsworth poem), although at times they can be misplaced or in a comatose state. In the movement from frolic to competitive athletics there is a continuum from spontaneous, animal-like activity to structured, rule-bound events wherein both the natural world and the world of everyday cultural activity is partially transcended. It is this partial transcendence that makes athletics a bit like art and religion, as we have seen Huizinga emphasize by way of appeal to Guardini. An athletic event can be, at least in principle, a limited perfection, if the oxymoron be permitted, a little piece of heaven here on earth.

In Feezell's own mind the greatest strength of the *Homo ludens* hypothesis is its phenomenological inclusiveness in that it can account for (*a*) aimless, frolicking play (of course); (*b*) competitive "pickup" athletic games that are nonetheless somewhat organized; and (*c*) highly organized athletic contests where external goods like power and nationalism and school pride and money play major roles (Feezell 2004a, 91–92). When *b* and *c* pinch the *Homo ludens* hypothesis, however, Keating's thesis is in the wings as either an alternative or at least ancillary hypothesis. Feezell's point, however, is moderate: one ought not to take athletic competition so seriously that the play element is lost. Perhaps the dispute between

Keating and Feezell can be put in the following terms: Keating *descriptively* alerts us to what can (or is likely to) occur in athletic competition, whereas Feezell, admitting that Keating is often correct at the descriptive level, nonetheless *prescriptively* asserts that athletics ought not to sever itself from its ludic roots (Feezell 2004a, 93). This prescription only makes sense against the background of an ancient Greek measure that still pulls at us today: the ideal of *sophrosyne*.

Another way to articulate the contrast between Keating and Feezell is to say that the former adopts a stance that could be called attitudinal parsimony: in some activities one plays, in others one competes to win. Period. The question is whether Keating's tidiness is bought at too great a price. I think the price is exorbitant in that its effect is to trivialize all of the best points made by Huizinga and Feezell. By way of (partial) contrast, Feezell's stance involves attitudinal complexity: one competes to win because it *is* an enjoyable, playful activity in its own right. Or, more precisely, the attitudinal complexity of the athlete is due to two sorts of seriousness, internal and external. That is, from an internal point of view, athletic competition is obviously taken very seriously by its participants and fans. However, from an external point of view, say, when viewed retrospectively in tranquility when the athletic event is a memory, we can see that it was only a game and ought not to have been taken too seriously. In the most reflective athletes, coaches, fans, and commentators, these two perspectives are precariously held together in a single glance. Feezell explicitly identifies his view as Aristotelian in this regard (Feezell 2004a, 93–94).

We are now in a position to appreciate Feezell's nonessentialist, yet nonnominalist, definition of sportsmanship in light of its purported phenomenological adequacy: "Sportsmanship is a mean between excessive seriousness, which misunderstands the importance of the spirit of play, and an excessive sense of playfulness, which might be called frivolity and which misunderstands the importance of victory and achievement when play is competitive. The good sport is both serious and nonserious. Many, if not most, examples of bad sportsmanship arise from an excessive seriousness" (Feezell 2004a, 95). Winning at all costs (and thus exhibiting hubris) is the most certain way to extinguish the play spirit. Or again, to turn athletics into a Hobbesian power struggle is to brutalize both the athletic event and us; we are dehumanized in the process (Schmitz 1979). Feezell is correct to notice that this focus on the attitude of the athlete has as a necessary corollary an attitude toward the opponent, an attitude that could (in the good sport) lead to mutual pursuit of *arete* but could also (in the poor sport) lead to taunting, cheating, and even deliberate dehumanization or a deliberate attempt to harm.

In Aristotelian fashion, we should only expect as much precision here in the definition of sportsmanship as the subject matter will bear (*Nicomachean Ethics* I.3). To see it as a mean between extremes is not to assume that it is an algorithm; but it *is* an ideal that can provide some guidance to the person of practical wisdom (*phronesis*), especially when this ideal is concretely exemplified in a particular athlete (e.g., the baseball player Edgar Martinez) who is universally acknowledged as a good sport.

4. WEISS, MACINTYRE, AND THE VIRTUOUS LIFE

It should now be clear that there is something myopic about the widely held dichotomy between the seriousness of life and philosophy, on the one hand, and the nonseriousness of athletic competition, on the other. Athletic competition is itself, in one sense and within conceptual bounds, serious. Feezell was awakened from his dogmatic slumbers in this regard by Weiss's groundbreaking book. However, whereas Weiss is the classic outsider to athletics, Feezell is the insider who knows what it is like to compete and nonetheless maintain an ironic distance with respect to such competition. It is precisely this ironic detachment that prevents Feezell from taking athletics *too* seriously, as seems to occur regularly in popular culture (Feezell 2004a, x, xiv).

Although there is considerable evidence on both sides to indicate that the athletics-as-pursuit-of-bodily-excellence hypothesis is at odds with the athletics-as-play hypothesis, I think that these two views are ultimately compatible; they mutually reinforce each other and can be brought into equilibrium. That is, the concepts of *arete* and *telos* emphasized by Weiss need not be seen (and should not be seen) as being at odds with Feezellian *sophrosyne*. Admittedly, Weiss is primarily interested in what can be seen as a Platonic search for *the* nature of athletics, whereas Feezell is primarily interested in the phenomenology of athletic competition. But Feezell admits that "I have little doubt that the pursuit of excellence is an important element in sports, but I have doubts about whether this is the element that *defines* the nature of sport" (Feezell 2004a, 4, emphasis added). Such a definition, he thinks, requires much more personal experience than Weiss brings to his analysis of athletics.

Why does athletic competition offer "to many people the context of their hopes, the locus of their momentary reprieve from a burdensome reality, or the repository for the only kind of heroism that they can appreciate at this moment in history"? (Feezell 2004a, 5). Presumably we cannot answer this question on the basis of the pursuit-of-bodily-excellence hypothesis. This is because Weiss's view does not help us understand much outside of, say, some competitions at the Olympic Games. What about city softball leagues, golf for hackers, after-work bowling, and pickup soccer games in South American slums? By claiming that the athletics-as-play hypothesis explains the phenomena in question better than the Weissian view, Feezell is not necessarily buying into essentialism. There is much to be learned from Frank McBride's Wittgenstein-inspired thesis that philosophers of athletics ought not to waste their time attempting to find an essentialist definition of athletics. However, to grant this much does not mean that a less ambitious sort of definition, based on overlapping properties of many different athletic activities, ought not to be sought (Feezell 2004a, 10; McBride 1979).

Even those who participate in athletics because they are paid to do so most likely started to play because of the intrinsic satisfaction of the activity. And even those who make a living by gambling on athletic events most likely enjoy viewing the athletic events that generate capital for them. On Feezell's account, even if athletic competitors do not seem to be playing their games, they are nonetheless "in the neighborhood" of play or they have a Wittgensteinian "family resemblance" to those who obviously do play their games. In different terms, despite the external goods that often drive athletic activity, there is always something autotelic about it if it is intrinsically enjoyable, as it surely is (Feezell 2004a, 11–14).

Although it would be hyperbolic to claim that training for an athletic event is *always* fun, it would also be misleading to run to the other (Weissian) extreme whereby the self-sacrifice of the athlete in training is seen as morbidly working against the sort of life that the athlete sees as extremely enjoyable. Actually I think that Feezell *is* being hyperbolic (even on the grounds of his own theory of moderation in athletics) in the following quotation, but as a rhetorical antidote to some of the excesses of the Weissian view he is surely on the mark: "It's neither winning nor even *how* you play that is most important; what is most important is simply *that* you play" (Feezell 2004a, 15; also Schacht 1973). Once again, I think that Weiss and Huizinga/Feezell can reach some sort of rapprochement: what athlete can remain utterly indifferent to the level of excellence of his or her performance? There is much to be said for a view of athletics as *both* teleologically oriented toward Weissian excellence *and* autotelically oriented toward Huizingian/Feezellian play.

It might be asked: who cares about how this debate between Weiss and Feezell is resolved when more pressing concerns, even more pressing concerns in philosophy of athletics, need to be addressed? Because it *does* matter how we talk about things, including athletic things, we should all care. Feezell's helpful analogy is as follows: when we call a controversial work of art pornography (or, by contrast, a masterpiece) we profoundly affect our attitude toward it. Likewise, (*a*) when we describe an athletic event as war we affect our attitude toward it in a nontrivial way, but (*b*) if we call it the pursuit of bodily excellence we are likely to have a different (indeed, a softer) attitude toward it, and (*c*) if we talk about it as a type of play we are more likely to discover the autotelic elements that are always there. In *c* we are also more likely to call to our attention the ironic distance that is required when we start to take athletics too seriously (Feezell 2004a, 17). Talk about athletics need not be cheap.

A difficult problem faces Feezell's view at this point. In order to avoid the reductionism of Weiss's view, wherein athletics is reduced to something external to it (bodily excellence), he has to emphasize the autotelic quality of athletics as play. But in order to defend the athletics-as-play thesis he calls upon the Aristotelian view that the virtuous character is centered on the ideal of moderation. The problem is this: how does

Feezell avoid compromising the autotelic, playful quality of athletics if athletics is turned into a tool for the purpose of a different external good, that is, character development? Feezell does not sidestep the problem in that he admits that the view of athletics as propaedeutic to character development is "part of the prevailing orthodoxy of the sports world" (Feezell 2004a, 123–124). Initially Feezell is ambivalent in his response to this problem. On the one hand, he does not want to threaten the autotelic quality of athletic competition; in any event, it is not obvious that athletic competition really *does* make us better people. On the other hand . . .

Feezell tries to respond to this problem by appeal to the virtue ethics approach taken by Alasdair MacIntyre. It is integral to MacIntyre's approach to emphasize that the virtues are never developed in the abstract but in *practices*. This point goes to the heart of MacIntyre's critique of modern moral theory in that philosophers have tended to debate incommensurable moral premises that are mere fragments dislodged from the historical context and shared lifeworld in which they originally made sense. This incommensurability leads many to conclude that our ultimate moral principles are arbitrary. MacIntyre is famous for contrasting the virtues of the Homeric warrior (e.g., *arete* as a cognate of the god of war, Ares), the Athenian citizen, the medieval person of faith aspiring for sainthood, the English gentleman or lady (as exemplified, say, in Jane Austen novels), and so on. Thankfully it will not be my task here to resolve long-standing and major issues in contemporary moral theory (Feezell 2004a, 126–127; MacIntyre 1984).

However, it is relevant to notice that among the practices mentioned by MacIntyre and Feezell are athletic practices like baseball and football. Each of these practices involves both internal and external goods. Among the external goods are fame, education, money, *and* character development. One of the goods internal to the practice of baseball is the ability of a catcher to throw out a runner who is trying to steal second base. This is a baseball virtue.

Although Feezell is not explicit on this point, if I understand him correctly he is suggesting a possible link between the virtues associated with the successful habituation to the intrinsic goods of a practice and the life of virtue in general. For example, those like Feezell who defend the character-building potential of athletic competition try to establish a link between the perseverance it takes to acquire the internal goods of a practice and the self-knowledge required in order to acquire them (as when a baseball player with a weak arm but a good glove knows that he or she is better suited to be a second baseman than to be a shortstop), on the one hand, and the virtues that serve one well in life in general, on the other. But Feezell is quick to point out that many other practices, with their different internal goods, would work as well, as in learning to become a craftsperson or a scientist or a musician. "The important thing is for young people to commit themselves substantially to *some* practice" (Feezell 2004a, 129).

There is a sense in which the courage, perseverance, and self-knowledge it takes to be a good X *could* serve one well in the effort to be a good person. But clearly there is no necessary connection here. To stick with baseball for a moment, it is well known that among the best players in the history of the game there have been individuals who were not terribly admirable as human beings: Ty Cobb, Joe DiMaggio, and Barry Bonds. The same, of course, could be said of the best composers or scientists or philosophers.

I assume that Feezell agrees that the virtues internal to a practice are only accidentally connected to the life of virtue in general. But I am not sure about this. He cites approvingly Iris Murdoch's (partially Hobbesian) view that human beings are basically defensive, touchy, and even selfish. Hence, what they need, on this philosophical anthropology, is a disciplined "unselfing." Murdoch's example is that of learning a foreign language, which draws us away from ourselves into a larger world of other cultures and ways of speaking and thinking (Feezell 2004a, 129–131; Murdoch 1971, 78–93).

Granted, athletic practices have the potential to unself an inflated ego; but they also have the potential to "Self!" an ego that was not previously inflated. I have more than once met individuals who were perfectly admirable people until they became aware of the fact in adolescence that they had athletic talent. Self-knowledge and lack of hubris are no easier to acquire in athletics than they are in other practices. To put the point bluntly, many athletes are not as good as they think they are, either as athletes or as people. And when they are idolized or paid exorbitant amounts of money, the problem gets worse. The external goods of fame and wealth can be such powerful lures that the athlete might even be tempted to win by cheating in order to get them (see Feezell 2005).

Here Feezell defends a counterintuitive claim (with the aid of Christopher Lasch) that I nonetheless think is correct. The degradation of athletics often occurs when athletic competition is (obviously) taken too seriously. But just as often such degradation occurs when the athletic competition itself is trivialized in the face of the pressures imposed by hegemonic external goods: fame, money, nationalism, school pride, and so on. Athletics is a fecund ground for philosophical examination if only because the subject matter is so subtle. Its degradation is just as often due to the fact that we do not take it seriously enough as it is due to our taking it too seriously (Feezell 2004a, 132–133; Lasch 1979, chap. 5).

In Feezell's language, winning, as an internal good to an athletic practice, is "significant" yet in proportion to other goods in life "trivial." A good double-switch by a National League baseball manager that leads to a win is not exactly the moral equivalent of a life-saving bone marrow surgery. The *telos* of an athlete involves the often difficult effort to incorporate the goods internal to an athletic practice into a wider lifelong narrative. MacIntyre describes this effort in medieval terms as a quest. The unity of a narrative quest is impeded when athletic fragments are blown out of their proper proportion. *The* good should take precedence over the lesser goods of a skillful corner kick in soccer or a deft Granby roll in wrestling. In a word, if and when athletes wonder about the good life, they become *philosophical* (Feezell 2004a, 133–136; MacIntyre 1984).

As before, there is no necessary connection here between internal athletic goods and virtues, on the one hand, and the good *life*, on the other. Many, perhaps most, athletes either ignore philosophical questions or treat them in the most banal way. The analogous unreflectiveness of most citizens, however, does not tarnish the activities of political philosophers; hence, philosophers of athletics need not be ashamed of their subject matter. A minimalist goal would be to not have athletes be *worse* human beings than they would be without their athletic activity. This is a real danger. Consider the famous sayings gathered by Feezell from the pantheon of football coaches:

> "I will demand a commitment to excellence and to victory, and that is what life is all about" (Vince Lombardi). "Winning isn't everything, but it beats anything that comes in second" (Paul Bryant). "Winning is living" (George Allen). "Every time you win, you're reborn; when you lose, you die a little" (George Allen). "No one ever learns anything by losing" (Don Shula). (Feezell 2004a, 137)

Several things can be noticed here. First, the Shula quote seems quite wrong, even from the point of view of one who is overly serious about athletics. Second, this list of dismal quotes does not contain the most notorious in the genre, Lombardi's (in)famous line about winning being the only thing that matters. And third, Feezell contrasts these coaches with another imaginary coach who thinks that it is wise to remind players that they are playing a relatively silly game in the light of life's tragedies, that they should not view athletics as war without the shooting, and that athletics should not be confused with what really matters in life. In real life this imaginary coach would probably be fired if he or she did not produce enough victories.

Unfortunately, it seems that we have to rest content with a "mixed moral result" from athletics. For example, some athletes will learn to lose gracefully, a virtue that transfers well to life in general, where setbacks, both minor and tragically major, are not infrequent. Other athletes (like John McEnroe) will never take responsibility for their defeats and will always find a way to blame others. By honestly admitting this mixed moral result, however, we will be taking an important step toward *understanding* the moral possibilities and pitfalls of athletics.

5. FREEDOM AND ABSURDITY

Feezell, like Michael Novak, has a faith in athletics that seeks understanding. There is no need to divorce interest in athletics from serious thought. But how *are* we to understand athletics? Thus far I have emphasized the Greek ideal of moderation (*sophrosyne*) in Feezell's account, but this is only part of Feezell's view. In this section I would like to emphasize two additional factors: freedom and absurdity (Feezell 2004a, 20; Novak 1976).

The version of freedom at work here is that of Frithjof Bergmann, wherein the athlete is free when he or she identifies with the athletic activity or has a strong sense of playful affirmation of the athletic activity: "As a [Weissian] spectator, it might be difficult to believe that the sweating, straining faces of pick-up basketball players express some deep sense of enjoyment and identification; but from the standpoint of the lived experience of the players, there is little doubt about this point" (Feezell 2004a, 23). Of course there are many other senses of "freedom" that are not being treated here. For example, to say that athletic activity is free in the sense mentioned above is not necessarily to say that the activity is chosen. Often we identify with our activities because we choose them, but just as often we choose to do things with which we do not identify, as in being civil to a colleague whom one detests. So also one might strongly identify with activities that are hardly chosen, as when someone is habituated to an athletic life at an early age by one's parents and culture, such that the individual in question engages in athletics because it is second nature to do so rather than the result of a choice (Bergmann 1977).

By thinking of freedom as identification rather than as choice, Feezell hopes to highlight the fact that athletes tend to see a match between their athletic activity and who they ought to be. To put the point in Pythagorean terms that heavily influenced Plato, they are *attuned* with, or are in *harmony* with, athletic activity. To be free is to be lighthearted. This is why it makes sense to say that people *play* football or soccer or golf. Seen in this light, play is not "puerile," as this term has been used previously, but is an important aspect of human authenticity (Feezell 2004a, 25).

We have been too much influenced, Feezell and Novak seem to say, by the Protestant and capitalist and Marxist idea that work is the only serious, important, and adult activity. The cliché "TGIF" seems to indicate a pervasive sense in popular culture that one must first work between Monday and Friday in order to deserve enjoyment of life on the weekend. This cliché follows quite easily from the Weberian thesis regarding the connection between the Protestant ethic and the spirit of capitalism. The

Homo ludens hypothesis contradicts this tendency: it is liberating play that is the *telos* of human life. (We have seen Huizinga cite Guardini favorably in this regard and regarding the connection between play and worship.) This crucial point is not lost on at least one basketball coach, Phil Jackson, even if it is lost on many others, including a great many in academe. Jackson encourages players (n.b.) to make their work play and their play work. That is, he encourages them both to enjoy their work and to take seriously their play. The greatest player whom he coached, Michael Jordan, was famous for working hard at, yet loving, practice time because it involved pure basketball, without external goods present to distract one away from the play spirit (Feezell 2004a, 26, 156; Jackson 1995, 123).

The fact that good health might be promoted by liberating athletic activity is ancillary to the play. Indeed, good health is yet another external good. The "animal joy" of the activity itself is what is crucial, a joy that is analogous to that experienced by schoolchildren who are released at recess. This exuberance continues even when the play in question is governed by rules. In effect, the liberating character of athletic activity is both freedom *from* (ennui or the overly serious) and freedom *to* (live authentically in an ironic play world that is both serious and nonserious, real and pretend). As before, this play world is not as accurately characterized by a Keating-like "either-or" as it is by a more complex "both-and" reflective equilibrium (Feezell 2004a, 27, 31; Schmitz 1979).

Despite the freedom experienced by athletes, Feezell wonders whether athletics is "absurd." We will need to be clear regarding what Feezell means by this word and also regarding how the possible absurdity of athletics is not an exception to (and, in fact, is a prime example of) his concern for Aristotelian moderation. In addressing these concerns it will be crucial once again to see athletics as being located in the tension between the nonserious and the serious. It is not unintelligible to see athletics as an insignificant diversion from real life or as a trivial amusement. The problem is that it is also not unintelligible to see it as an activity that transforms ordinary experience into something more structured and meaningful, much like a work of art does so.

As a first approximation of an adequate response to the issue of the absurdity of athletics, Feezell compares the athlete to Sisyphus in a

Camus-like way. In that nothing comes of the competitive play in athletics (one inning after another, one spring training after another, etc.), just as nothing comes of Sisyphus's efforts with the rock, one is tempted to say that the absurdity of athletics might lie in "the incongruity between human purposiveness and necessary frustration" (Feezell 2004a, 48).

But Feezell ultimately rejects the thesis that athletics is absurd *if* absurdity is understood in Sisyphean terms. Whereas Sisyphus is bored with his task, athletes are hardly bored with their athletic activity. Evidence for this claim can be found in the fact that whereas Sisyphus performed his task involuntarily on the command of the gods, athletes tend to voluntarily play their games. Further, we have seen that athletes are liberated through their games into a region of authentic activity seldom found in ordinary life. Finally, whereas there is no end to Sisyphus's labor, there is a *telos* to each athletic game; there is something at issue that gives the athletic activity consummatory, rather than merely instrumental, value (Feezell 2004a, 49–50; Camus 1955).

The absurdity of athletic play is better understood, Feezell thinks, in terms of Thomas Nagel's version of the absurd. Camus's Sisyphean absurdity arises not in a human person or in an irrational world, but in the relationship between the two, specifically in the incongruity between human aspiration and the recalcitrant reality that we confront. Nagel's absurd, by way of partial contrast, consists in a collision *within ourselves* between the seriousness with which we take our projects in life and the ever-present possibility of taking our projects as open to doubt. That is, we act as if our activities are all that matter, but there is always a point of view from which this seriousness seems either gratuitous or silly. It is when these two viewpoints collide that athletics seems absurd. The absurd that arises in us is a function of our ability to disengage ourselves in reflection. This reflective detachment, it should be noted, has a long history in the classics of spirituality (variously called *adiaphoria* by the Stoics, *nada* by Saint John of the Cross, indifference by Saint Ignatius of Loyola, or the no self doctrine in certain Buddhists, etc.).

The Nagelian point to recognizing the absurdity of athletics is not to abandon athletic practices, but to return to them with a healthy sense of irony. "Our seriousness would be mediated by an ironic sense of our own limitations and an unconvinced retreat from dogmatic claims of ultimacy." (I wonder if Feezell means "should" here rather than "would.") Or again, in an allusion to Wordsworth ("The World Is Too Much with Us"), he suggests that "an ironic sense of detachment never allows the world to be too much with us" (Feezell 2004a, 53; Nagel 1979). The picture one gets is the following: the athlete receives a momentary reprieve from the burdens of everyday reality in his or her play, but in moments of reflective detachment we notice the unreality of the play world, a realization that the play world—perfect as it may be in its own right—is nonetheless inferior to the real world. But the admission that athletic competition is absurd is not meant to negate the care, even devotion that passes into rapture, that athletes and fans have for their practices. The absurdity of athletics requires that we notice *both* the seriousness and the nonseriousness of play: "We play our games with abandon and intensity as if nothing mattered more than making this basket, winning this game, overcoming this challenge. Yet this attitude of seriousness is undermined by the reflection that insists it is 'only a game'" (Feezell 2004a, 54). Once again, Feezell's Nagelian absurdity not only is not opposed to Aristotelian moderation, it is an extension of it to athletics.

Without a serious pursuit of victory, the competitive play found in athletics would degenerate into mere frolic. And without ironic detachment from such serious pursuit of victory, the competitive play found in athletics would degenerate into single-minded overseriousness. Even if Nagel is wrong about the absurdity of life in general—I think he is, whereas Feezell seems to think Nagel is correct—there is much to be said in favor of Nagelian absurdity when dealing with competitive play. In different terms, I think that Feezell is correct about the local absurdity of competitive play and the corresponding need for irony here, even if I am not *deeply ironic* about life in general, as is Feezell. But in order to spell this out a wider project in philosophy of religion would have to be engaged (see Dombrowski 2004, 2005, 2006).

In an ironic approach to athletics we should be willing to criticize two cliches: "Winning is not the most important thing; it's the only thing"; and "It's not whether you win or lose, but how you play the game." The former pushes us toward Aristotelian *agrios* or *skleros*, as defined above.

And the latter pushes us toward Aristotelian *homolochos* by utterly trivializing the pursuit of victory; such pursuit is a legitimate *aspect* of athletic activity. The task for the philosopher of athletics is to avoid all such partial truths. My only complaint with Feezell in this regard is his attempt to move beyond the local absurdity of competitive play to the global absurdity of life in general. I am not convinced that "life is to be played," in the absurd sense Feezell has in mind; but I hope my stance here does not necessarily mean that I have capitulated to "the despair of *homo gravis*" (Feezell 2004a, 57, 77).

Before he died, Weiss was able to respond to Feezell on this point, and the response is quite instructive. If we are asked, "Is there something absurd about athletics?" Weiss thinks that we should respond by saying that *anything* could be seen as absurd if viewed from an alien position. That is, no area (not even violence or massacre) can be hermetically sealed off from the efforts of ironists or satirists. Those who Socratically seek to understand athletics should know that various contemporary Aristophanes have their baskets ready (although there are baskets waiting for the ironists and satirists, too).

Thus, it might seem that Weiss is like Feezell in being a global absurdist or a global ironist. But Weiss would have us notice that "what is needed is a recognition of the strengths and limits of both the mean and the extremes" (Weiss 1995a, 657–658). If I understand him correctly, Weiss is defending only local absurdity or local irony. He is saying that taking human life as a whole seriously is a more weighty affair than taking athletic activity seriously. Or again, not being serious enough about life in general is a worse vice than not taking athletics seriously enough. At times (when he does not flirt with global irony) Feezell correctly concedes the point Weiss is making here.

Thus far I have made two main points about Feezell's stance regarding the absurdity of athletics. Regarding the *nature* of the absurd Feezell rightly focuses on Nagel's version of the absurd rather than on Camus's more histrionic version conducive to heroic defiance. However, regarding the *scope* of the absurd he pushes beyond the local absurdity of athletics and some other particular practices and sometimes argues (unpersuasively, I think) for global absurdity, the absurdity of human life in general.

A less hegemonic ironism would be more appropriate, I think. It is one thing to say that we ought not to take games like basketball too seriously; it is quite another to say that we ought not to take family life, our children's health, or our overall goals in life too seriously.

Feezell is most persuasive when he talks about the local absurdity of athletics, in particular. Athletes and coaches (e.g., Bill Parcells) who exhibit no irony whatsoever in their attitude toward athletics, those for whom athletics *is* life, strike us as immoderate. Likewise regarding those who trivialize the pursuit of bodily excellence and achievement by seeing athletics as "the toy department of life" (Feezell 2004a, 58). The issue at hand is one instance of the more general philosophical problem that concerns the subjective and the objective. From the inside, competitive play is felt as extremely important by the athlete, fan, or coach, but from an objective point of view, called the "view from nowhere" by Nagel, we get a quite different assessment. How are we to reconcile these two different perspectives? (Nagel 1986).

One should manage one's philosophical expectations here. Although it makes sense to try to reconcile subjectivity and objectivity in our view of athletics, by calling athletics "absurd" we are saying that we should, in part, rest content with a "proper perplexity." But some responses to this perplexity are better than others. One very promising response opened up by Nagel is to say that the distinction between the subjective and the objective is a matter of degree. It is the same human person who, on the one hand, cares intensely about the outcome of an athletic event but who, on the other hand, looks on his or her intensity of belief with ironic distance. One can imagine a continuum of points of view from intense self-absorption, at one end, to complete disembodiment and objectivity, at the other. For example, note how in popular discourse we tend to tell a parent who is angry that his child is not getting enough playing time on the local high school football team to "step back" or to "get some distance" on the situation (Feezell 2004a, 59–62).

However much Feezell encourages us to take the impersonal, objective point of view, wherein our prejudices (literally prejudgments) are held in check, he also wants us to preserve our intensely subjective feelings, including an intense love of athletic competition. *Something* worthwhile is revealed in subjective intensity, even if this something must be held in check by an abstract point of view (the view from nowhere) wherein objectivity is made possible. As I write in the spring of 2008, I confess that *my* life (which is now lived in Seattle) is enhanced by the hope that the Mariners will have a strong team this year. Am I wrong in caring about how the Mariners perform? However strange it seems to care about these things (strange even to me when I adopt a more objective point of view), I *do* care about them. My life, in part, is about how the Mariners do. And I thank Feezell for giving me the courage to say so (Feezell 2004a, 63–65).

But athletics is only part of the picture, whether my own subjective picturing or an objective picture of who I am. Hence, I remain unconvinced by Feezell's efforts to globalize absurdity. It just seems much more difficult for me to think that I could take family matters, life-and-death matters, too seriously than it is for me to think that I could take athletic matters too seriously. Actually the latter effort is not that hard at all when one of *life's* setbacks is before me. Once again, Feezell himself sometimes seems to acknowledge the difficulty with global absurdity when he cites the following examples: "The young player strikes out with the bases loaded and the team loses the Big Game. Someone attempts to console the distraught young person: 'It's only a game.' Death or illness in the family causes a player to miss a practice or game. Poor academic performance causes athletic suspension. The demands of a job force someone to forgo the big softball tournament. Someone is severely injured in a game. The other stunned players look on and later say 'Something like this shows what's really important.' A national tragedy puts sports in 'proper perspective'" (Feezell 2004a, 66–67). As Wordsworth puts the point, there are some things that are "too deep for tears" (from the last line of "Intimations of Immortality from Recollections of Early Childhood").

It will be remembered that Weiss holds that, just as Aristophanes in his play *The Clouds* lampooned Socrates by having the actor "playing" Socrates be put in a basket that was elevated over the stage so as to simulate the heavens, so also it is easy to put athletes in baskets, as Feezell realizes: "Putting a little ball in a small hole in the ground some distance away [golf]. Carrying a leather ball to a point many yards away [North American football, roughly similar to rugby]. Hitting a thrown ball with the intention of allowing one to run around in a circle, arriving at precisely the point from which one starts! [baseball, roughly similar to cricket]. . . . From the standpoint of everyday life, games are by their very nature rather silly" (Feezell 2004a, 68). Clearly there is a difference in degree. It is much harder to put a parent in a satirist's or ironist's basket if the parent cares deeply for the health of a child. But in kind? I think so. Or at least the following should be urged: some differences in degree are so wide that they become, for practical purposes, differences in kind.

Life is not absurd, as I see things (cf. Feezell 2004a, 57, 70, 77), although I admit that some sort of Stoic or Neoplatonist or religious detachment is required even regarding those concerns that are most serious. Otherwise we would *never* overcome grief. I also admit that at different points in my life I have been tempted by the global ironist's stance. But the following sort of comment from Nagel, seemingly endorsed by Feezell, is a real puzzle: "Watching the human drama is a bit like watching a Little League baseball game: the excitement of the participants is perfectly understandable but one can't really enter into it" (Nagel 1986, 217–218; Feezell 2004a, 72). Some people, at least, *do* enter into the excitement of the human drama with a Bergsonian élan vital or a Zorba-like zest.

Confined to the local absurdity of athletics, however, I find Feezell most instructive. He is correct that the problem is that of "coherent attitudes" (Feezell 2004a, 70), although I would prefer the Rawlsian language of "reflective equilibrium" that must be reached between the subjective and the objective. Something is wrong with a view of athletics that does not do justice to both of these perspectives. It is very easy to slip into disequilibrium when we take athletics too seriously or not seriously enough, as the ancient Greeks realized long ago. In this regard our problem with athletics is not much different from the one they confronted.

What is new and exciting in Feezell's approach is the clarity with which he formulates two key components that must be brought into reflective equilibrium: one needs to be simultaneously (or at least sequentially) athletic participant and observer. "It is like sitting in the stands watching the game and judging it to be trivial while at the same time playing or coaching with utmost seriousness, playing or coaching *as if* it really mattered" (Feezell 2004a, 72). For the conscientious the chief problem is that of preserving subjective immediacy, but I assume that the more general problem in popular athletic culture is that participants and fans are either forgetful of, or worse, utterly ignorant of, the objective assessment of athletics (Feezell 2004a, 73). The goal is to live with a sort of grace and self-command while affirming both relevant perspectives.

The irony involved here enables one to engage in competitive play *as if* it really mattered; hence, there is not as wide a gap as might initially seem to exist between athletic play and the theatrical play of an actor. Method actors, in particular, can, like athletes, easily get caught up in, and hence lost in, their play. Feezell labels competitive play "serious nonseriousness" or "nonserious seriousness." Given his defense of global absurdity, he sometimes treats these two labels as equivalent (Feezell 2004a, 74, cf. 152). But given what I have said above, I think the former label more accurately represents athletics. The important thing is to have one's athletic engagement held in check by objective detachment and one's objective detachment modified by athletic engagement (Feezell 2004a, 74; Feinberg 1984).

It might seem that Feezell's defense of the virtue of humility is at odds with Aristotle's moderation in that, on Nietzschean grounds, humility is a Christian virtue that has no ancient equivalent. Not exactly. By "humility" Feezell means a moderation between what Nagel calls "nihilistic detachment and blind self-importance." That is, humility in Feezell's quite defensible usage is a type of Aristotelian moderation that requires a sort of self-knowledge very much in the tradition of the ancient imperative *Gnothi seauton* (Know yourself!). It is to Feezell's credit that he points out a family resemblance among modern (or postmodern) irony, humility, and certain ancient Greek ideals (Feezell 2004a, 74–75; Nagel 1986, 222).

In fact, all of the cardinal virtues from Plato's *Republic* are required for an athlete to be virtuous. Moderation, as we have seen, is crucial. But courage (*andreia*) is also needed when athletes confront isolation and failure, as inevitably they must (Corlett 2002). Questions of justice (*dike*) also abound, especially because athletics is rule-bound activity: Do professional athletes deserve their large salaries? Should communities spend large amounts of money for sports stadia? On children's athletics teams should the best players perform the most or does every member of the team deserve equal playing time? Should a successful designated hitter be allowed to enter the baseball Hall of Fame?. And the whole point to discussing the absurd in athletics is to elicit in athletes, coaches, and fans their latent potential for *sophia*, for wisdom (Feezell 2004a, 76; Feezell and Clifford 1997, 17).

The following objection can be imagined: concern for virtue will tend to dull the competitive edge in the athlete, so it is better to deemphasize such concern as long as winning is a crucial part of athletic competition. Feezell thinks that this objection leads to what he calls the "Kierkegaardian competitor." Just as Kierkegaard thought that faith excluded objective reflection, so also the Kierkegaardian competitor must be infinitely committed to winning, undeflected by rational considerations. Feezell's response to this objection is telling. The "ironic competitor," in contrast to the Kierkegaardian one, is not listless or halfhearted. Rather, he or she is *wise*. That is, there is no reason to think that athletes need to be excluded from the ranks of the reflective merely because they compete to win. "It is not as if the ironic competitor must continually mutter to herself, 'Sport is absurd, sport is absurd,' as she shoots every jumper or fields every ground ball" (Feezell 2004a, 78–79).

By coming to understand athletics better we do not thereby dry up our competitive juices in that as (Aristotelian) rational animals we are naturally fit—with large brains relative to body size and large cerebral cortices relative to brain size—to *think* while, or at least immediately after, we compete. And the consideration that we are rational animals is further reason to be skeptical about global absurdity. The maniacal (Kierkegaardian) competitor and the crazed fan, who know nothing of moderation, are hardly worthy models for us to follow.

6. SOME PRACTICAL RESULTS

The above accounts of sportsmanship and the absurd enable us to easily reach equilibrium with respect to several intuitions that reflective people have shared since the time of the ancient Greeks and their use of the *rhabdos*. For example, it is easy to see why cheating in athletics is wrong in that it would be an indication that we took athletics too seriously. (There are also some obvious and legitimate deontological, social contract, and utilitarian objections to cheating.) When disequilibrium occurs, we need to check either our intuitions or our arguments to determine the cause of the disequilibrium, but no such crisis occurs with respect to cheating on the moderate view of athletics as competitive play.

As we have seen Aristotle notice, however, we should expect only as much precision as the subject matter allows, and determining which athletic actions *are* examples of cheating, of intentionally gaining an unfair advantage over one's opponent, is difficult. For example, Feezell is too permissive, I have come to think, when he suggests that throwing a spitball in professional baseball is not cheating, but is rather an infraction that is "part of the game," like a moving pick in basketball. That is, because of an opposition to *deliberate* breaking of the rules in athletics, I have come to disagree with Feezell when he says that cheating only occurs in the extreme cases (Feezell 2004a, 108). It is the *concept* of cheating, rather than its application, that is illuminated by Feezell's overall view (also Lehman 2002; Loland 2002). That is, it seems to me that cheating is common in athletics, even in high school golf competitions and pickup basketball games, where one might assume otherwise.

This view of athletics as competitive play also enables one to easily handle the conceptual issue regarding blowouts. Granted, in contrast to Weiss, Feezell thinks that there is nothing *humiliating* in losing an athletic event. (For example, I have been on the losing end thousands of times and I remain buoyant). Nonetheless, on Feezell's usage, there can be something *embarrassing* involved if one loses badly. The nature of competition as a struggle *with* (rather than against) an opponent would work against running up the score on a weaker party. Here the silver rule is instructive: do not do to others what you would not want done to you (Feezell 2004a, 116; Dixon 1992).

In addition to enabling us to understand better the inappropriateness of cheating and blowouts, Feezell also enables us to better understand the locution "respect for the game." Athletic competition takes place within *historical* practices. The practice of baseball, say, goes back to the nineteenth-century figure Abner Doubleday (or perhaps even earlier), while other athletic practices can be traced back to the ancient Greeks. We should not ignore the fact that there is thus a community not only of present practitioners of these practices, but of those practitioners who have gone before. Here we should notice that there are certain internal goods that are essential to the historical practice in question (e.g., skating well in hockey) that ought to be cherished, in contrast to those "goods" that are accidental additions to the practice in question (e.g., fighting in professional hockey, almost entirely absent in college hockey) that are best left behind.

I should close this chapter with further explanation regarding why I am more favorably disposed to Huizinga's synoptic view *sub specie ludi* than I am to Feezell's view of global absurdity. The two are not equivalent in large measure because of Huizinga's theism and Feezell's agnosticism. The ecstatic quality of play, its ability to take one out of one's normal place so as to reside at least temporarily in some higher (Platonic) realm, is characteristic of Huizinga's approach, which clearly has an upward, indeed a theistic, trajectory as he moves from lower to higher types of play. By contrast, Feezell moves from the ease with which even lovers of athletics can doubt whether athletic contests amount to a hill of beans in the ultimate scheme of things to a doubt regarding whether there really is an ultimate scheme of things. Along with Huizinga I think that human existence is ludic, but it need not be absurd. This view is nonetheless compatible with Feezell's careful argumentation in favor of the claim that athletics, in particular, is both ludic and absurd.

Earlier I gestured toward the theoretical issues in philosophy of religion that are involved in my skepticism regarding global absurdity (see Dombrowski 2004, 2005, 2006). But the differences are also practical, and for two reasons. First, belief in global absurdity seems to depend in part on an ironic *disposition* that is largely outside of rational control and is at odds with Huizinga's dispositional optimism. For example, Feezell frequently indicates that life tends to be burdensome or boring; hence the *need* to escape from it in the safe world of athletics. No doubt Feezell accurately describes why some people find athletics so attractive. But others, I suppose, find it attractive along with everything else in life that is intrinsically valuable. That is, the sort of lighthearted liberation that Feezell rightly finds in athletics can also be found in other aspects of life. Some people find life in general intoxicating.

Second, my problems with global absurdity are also due, in part, to my practical inability to make sense of certain ways of speaking that would be required if one held global absurdity. It seems entirely appropriate to say to a friend who has lost an athletic event, even a big athletic event, that "it's just a game." But it does not seem appropriate, indeed it seems odious and reprehensible, to say to a friend who has just had a death in the family that "it's just a life." One pays too great a price, as I see things, for accepting the second locution as well as the first. In effect, by accepting the second locution we would put too many other cherished beliefs in disequilibrium with each other.

I am claiming that philosophers of athletics should remain humble and not give in to hubris by thinking that by trying to understand athletics they have an insider's advantage in the greater game of life. This "greater game" is metaphorical, at best, and produces the most invidious sorts of disequilibrium. As Feezell himself often notes, trying to understand *athletics* is noble work in its own right. This work ought to include an appropriation of Aristotle's claim (*Nicomachean Ethics* 1128A–B) that it is essential to *phronesis* to steer a dexterous (*epidexios*) yet buoyant (*eutrapelos*) course between the boorish and morose (*agriokoi kai skleroi*) life of *homo gravis* and the overly playful (*paidias*) life of buffoons (*phortikoi*).

The Process of Becoming Virtuous

I. INTRODUCTION

It has been the purpose of the present book to take what might seem to be static ancient Greek ideals and put them in motion in contemporary philosophic thought about athletics. In previous publications I tried to do the same for supposedly static ancient Greek ideals and contemporary philosophy of religion (Dombrowski 2004, 2005, 2006).

This last chapter of the book will highlight this dynamism, as well as the dynamism involved in the life of virtue. In this regard the athletics-as-pursuit-of-bodily-excellence hypothesis will be considered precisely as dynamic. For example, two sorts of process (atomic and transitional) will be examined in the effort to highlight the dynamic character of the view of athletics as the pursuit of bodily excellence.

This processual view of the pursuit of bodily excellence is grounded in a positive sense of athletic asceticism (almost a redundancy) indebted to Plotinus. This affirmation of asceticism is at odds with the Nietzschean (and now popular) view of asceticism as world negating and mortifying. Rather, as Saint Ignatius of Loyola noted as late as the sixteenth century, physical and spiritual "exercises" are analogous (St. Ignatius of Loyola 1951, "Introductory Observations"). Likewise, "asceticism" and "ethics" interpenetrate with each other in that both of these words have their roots in athletic training, as a consideration of Plotinus will make clear.

Dynamism is integral not only to the athletics-as-pursuit-of-bodily-excellence hypothesis, but to the *Homo ludens* hypothesis as well. To say that human life is characterized by the ludic is not to say that it is absurd. Athletics provides for us both playful atomic experiences that are intrinsically valuable and transitions from one athletic experience to the next. These transitions facilitate the sort of narrative structure required to find meaning in life. That is, life need not be one damned thing after another even if it is, at times, tragic.

Contemporary defenses of "aretism" or "Olympism," especially through the work of Mike McNamee, point the way forward toward a defensible philosophical view of what athletics is and ought to be. The inspiration here is found in the Greek ideals that are the subjects of the present book, even if these ideals have thus far been realized in practice only partially. Further, agent-centered traits will be crucial if we hope to more fully realize these ideals in the future.

Having "a sense of fair play" and "playing by the rules" are crucial both for the virtuous athlete and for the virtuous citizen. In this regard we can perhaps hope for a (Rawlsian) realistic utopia wherein our nascent sense of what athletics both is and should be can go hand in glove with our nascent sense of what is involved in the process of creating a just society.

2. DYNAMIC HYLOMORPHISM

In order to explicate the processual nature of the effort to make one's life *as an athlete* virtuous (in contrast to making the athletic *life* virtuous, which seems to take athletics too seriously, as I see things), it will be worth our while to return to certain features of Weiss's view.

No one, not even a Cartesian, can totally identify with his or her mind, in that we are embodied beings; likewise regarding total identification with one's body in that we are also thinking beings. Along with Aristotle we can still say that we are thinking animals. It is not redundant to call attention here to the obvious: our bodies are living, organic entities. This is in contrast to Julien Offray de La Mettrie and his legacy as continued by modern mechanists, who see human bodies as machines. To call the heart a pump is to use a metaphor, rather than to speak a literal truth. We *should* take the body seriously, but not when it is (misleadingly) conceived as a machine. Alfred North Whitehead's classic *Science and the Modern World*, congenial in many respects to Weiss's process orientation, stands as a bulwark against the mechanization of the human body (Whitehead 1925).

It is true that we can temporarily be lost in our bodies in athletic competition, and that at other times bodily demands can be "imperious" (say, when we are ill), but thinking beings cannot totally *identify* themselves with their bodies any more than they can do so with their minds. We are hylomorphs whose integration of body and mind is always at least partially achieved, but full integration can be approached only asymptotically. Our emotions, in particular, tend to bring about a fusion of body and mind in that they are themselves at once both bodily and mental. Athletics, on this account, involves the controlled expression of emotion and hence involves an ideal means whereby unified persons (Weiss says "men") can be forged. Or again, our bodies alone, even athletic bodies that are excellent, reveal who we are only in part; likewise, one cannot live a life of the mind for very long without bodily demands intruding (Weiss 1969, 37–39). The ethical ideal appropriate for dynamic hylomorphism is, as before, *kalokagathia*.

The mathematical concept of a "vector" can be used to suggest that a mindbody has a direction that connects the present with a possible future or a future held in prospect. Simple organisms have a vector that is largely unsupervised, but our bodies can have vectors that are highly planned and stretched out over a very long time, with the mind correcting the vectorial thrust of the mindbody when it misses the mark (a literal *hamartia*). Athletic training (in partial contrast to mere conditioning, which involves far less of an intellectual element) allows the athlete to become more fully his or her body and to become habituated to the appropriate athletic skills. Once again, this process can never be complete, in that when the body resists us (say, when we are tired), we are acutely aware of the fact that there is at least a notional distinction between mind and body. But a well-trained athletic hylomorph can engage in a mental and bodily act like the swing of a baseball bat "all at once," as it were (Weiss 1969, 40–47).

The moral function of a coach is to draw out or to educe what is latent in the athlete so that the athlete's *telos* can be more fully achieved, which leads to a sort of vicarious achievement on the part of the coach, too. That is, to evaluate the coach primarily or exclusively in terms of winning percentage or conference championships is a perversion from the perspective of virtue ethics. While the athlete, especially the young athlete, might have a tendency to have a myopic view of time, the coach, who is possibly older and wiser, should be able to more easily see the athlete's challenges from a wider temporal perspective. By tracing the athlete's historical influences and assessing his or her present abilities, the coach can help the young athlete to imagine where current athletic activity might be leading in the overall vectorial course of life. And the coach can also be especially instrumental in encouraging the athlete to commit to a change of course if the vectorial thrust into the future looks ominous—say, if an athlete with mediocre talent plans to make a living some day as a professional athlete (Weiss 1969, 48–50, 60–63).

The issue is tricky, however, in that the athlete should not sell himself or herself short, say, by failing to dedicate sufficiently to training or by giving up prematurely (Weiss 1969, 64–68). We will see that Plotinus is still instructive today regarding athletic *askesis*. Weiss puts the Aristotelian and Plotinian point well: "By going through comparable acts again and again under controlled conditions, he builds up the power of quickly estimating what a situation demands and how he is to behave in it. Without the habit, he will be forced to spend too much time in deliberating or experimenting when he has to be right, fast" (Weiss 1969, 90). The wise athlete negotiates fluidly between habitual rhythms and opportunistic flexibility. In some athletic events (e.g., the shot put) habitual rhythms dominate, whereas in others flexibility is crucial.

Time is also crucial. Although in the abstract, time can be seen as a continuum that is infinitely divisible, concretely it is not lived as a continuous flow, but in terms of a sequence of distinct moments, as in the "all at once" character mentioned above in the swing of a baseball bat. Athletic contests are composed of a nested series of these "presents": pitches, innings, punches, rounds, quarters, halves, periods, and so on. In Bergsonian fashion we should notice the dramatic difference between the mechanical and uniform nature of clock time and time as experienced in an athletic event. A lopsided game or one repeatedly interrupted by commercial messages can seem to last forever, whereas a well-played one can seem to fly by in an instant, like a one-hundred-meter dash. Great quarterbacks in football are said to have the ability to "slow things down" in their heads when dozens of things happen at once in a crucial play. Further, in endurance contests the event seems to go on forever, but that is the very point of an endurance event: who can go on "forever" at the fastest pace? (Weiss 1969, 114–123). But it is morally questionable whether endurance events should push human beings beyond the limits of what (most) human beings can endure and still achieve *eudaemonia*. Like some forms of boxing, endurance events become problematic if death is a predictable result. For example, nine people have died in the London Marathon since its inception in 1981.

Weiss puts the point regarding the athletic "present" in apt terms: "In sport the largest present is the present of the game. In this we can isolate plays and moves only conceptually. The bunt and any other play is an organic, integral factor in the present indivisible whole of the game. The plays are, of course, also distinct units—as are the moves they encompass—each with its own present. There is no more mystery here than there is in the fact that I am an individual with inalienable rights and duties, and also an integral part of a family having its own rights and duties" (Weiss 1969, 164). One wonders, however, why the same logic could not be used to talk about the present season, or the present career of a star player, or any number of other "presents."

Spencer Wertz does an excellent job of making explicit the processual nature of athletic training and competition. And he does this in reference to Weiss's philosophy of athletics, especially in reference to Weiss's later essays, written after his groundbreaking book, in spite of the fact that Weiss insists that he is not a process philosopher. Wertz's key contribution lies in noticing two processes going on in athletics. The first is atomic in character and is analogous to what process thinkers call actual occasions or events. In athletics these would be individual plays (or individual strides, say, in a race). Like temporal moments, these can be *theoretically* analyzed into parts (Whitehead's "stages of concrescence"), as in the beginning of a swing, the contact with the ball, the follow through, and so on. But in reality these parts occur so quickly that they are, in a way, indivisible quanta. They occur, but from a *practical* point of view they do not become (Wertz 1995; Weiss 1980, 1981, 1982; Whitehead 1925, 1978).

The second sort of process occurs in what process philosophers call a "transition" from one play (or stride) to the next. Here there is genuine becoming as one play (or stride) is followed by another until eventually the game (or race) is over. In a broader (and hence weaker) sense one game is followed by another until eventually the season or an athletic career is over. Both processes—atomic and transitional—occur together in an athletic contest, although "the great moments" in athletics tend to be individual plays, which are like Wordsworthian "spots of time."

Each new game (or season) brings new play events. For the athlete and fan this is an endless source of joy; for those not much interested in athletics it brings a sense that, to paraphrase Wordsworth: "Sports are too much with us. Late and soon, sitting and watching—mostly watching on television—we lay waste our powers of identification and enthusiasm and, in time, attention as more and more closing rallies and crucial putts and late field goals and final playoffs and sudden deaths and world records and world championships unreel themselves ceaselessly before our half-lidded eyes" (Angell 1985, 147). Whatever one's assessment of athletic novelty, however, there is the realization both that athletic plays and games (and seasons) have temporal duration and that the games (and seasons) have an internal developmental pattern that is best traced in narrative form.

The prominence of concepts like process, emergence, development, transition, fluidity, and so on, makes it possible to say that athletics involves a sort of staunch opposition to static concepts. Athletics involves hylomorphs *in motion*. Or again, in a very abstract way rules define the character of athletic games, but it is the *energy* of particular athletes that really brings them into existence. Once in existence, these dynamic processes are societal entities nested in Russian doll fashion (e.g., plays inside of innings, innings inside of games, games inside of seasons, seasons inside of careers or franchise histories, franchise histories inside of national histories, etc.).

Myopia is possible at every stage of process, as in the tendency to gloat after a great play when one's team is still behind in the game as a whole, or as in the tendency to gloat after a great game when the season still has a long way to go (Wertz 1995, 2002). The most egregious sort of myopia, and not a rare one, is that of the athlete who had a glorious career as a youth failing to see how this moment fits into life in general. For example, this ex-athlete might succumb to alcoholic self-pity when remembering the glory days. The *life* of an athlete can be tragic even if athletic losses are not.

3. ASCETICISM AS ATHLETIC TRAINING IN PLOTINUS

It will be useful at this point to accentuate the implicit asceticism found in the training process of most athletes. Indeed, Viktor Frankl sees athletics as "the asceticism of today" (Frankl 1978). In this regard Plotinus will be our guide. Then we will consider the process dimensions of the *Homo ludens* hypothesis.

At least as far back as Aristotle, and probably before, it was a commonplace in ancient Greek culture to consider that virtue consisted in a mean between two extremes. Moderation (*sophrosyne*) was a key virtue, perhaps the key virtue, consisting in a mean between self-indulgence (loosely, *pleonexia*), or thinking too much of oneself and one's desires, on the one hand, and thinking too little of oneself and one's needs (loosely, *mikropsychia*), on the other. In that advanced economies tend to encourage pleonexic tendencies, it is not too surprising that many recent interpreters of late ancient philosophy see the asceticism that characterizes many thinkers in this period either as an example of *mikropsychia* or as an embarrassing feature for which one must give an apologia. My thesis in this section is that defenders of Plotinus need not be embarrassed by his asceticism and that asceticism need not be a type of *mikropsychia*. Integral to this thesis will be an emphasis on the athletic nature of *askesis*.

There is a difference between moderation and penance. The former consists in denying ourselves what is excessive, luxurious, flashy, superfluous; that is, eliminating what we might want to have as opposed to what we really need as an athlete or as a person. But penance consists in denying ourselves what is essential for us to have; it does not eliminate that which is excessive but that which is integral to our well-being. In which category is asceticism to be placed? In order to answer this question one must realize that the etymology of the word *askesis* shows an athletic origin, as evidenced in Liddell and Scott. The word refers not so much to self-denial as to the practice or training required to compete in an athletic event. Although the word *askesis* eventually came to be associated with the penitential way of life, it must be emphasized that ascetic training is also needed to avoid *pleonexia* so as to obtain moderation. Or as Porphyry implies (*De abstinentia* I, 31), asceticism enables us to escape from barbarism so that we might "enter the stadium naked and unclothed, striving for the most glorious of all prizes, the Olympia of the soul."

A. H. Armstrong is certainly correct in noting that the deepest tension in Plotinus's thought deals with two opposing valuations of the movement from unity to multiplicity, but tension is not the same as incoherence (Armstrong 1940). The "descent" of the individual soul into a body is both a fall and a compliance with what is required for there to be besouled agency at all. The world is both a prison for souls and necessary for their flourishing. If the soul selfishly devotes itself to the body it becomes entrapped in atomistic particularity; thus, the root defect of soul is self-isolation. But the mere fact of being joined with an athletic body does not necessarily imply imprisonment. Through purification (*katharsis*) and training (*askesis*) we can gain a foothold in what is really real.

It is well known that soul for Plotinus is dual. He uses Aristotle's notion of soul as the immanent form of the body as a starting point from which to develop his own somewhat different doctrine of the rational soul as the true human or the human within. Yet Armstrong rightly notes that Plotinus captures the true Platonic otherworldliness, as opposed to its bastardization, in seeing the material universe in its goodness, beauty, and unity as the best possible image of the intelligible. Thus, the cleavage in human nature for Plotinus is not between matter and spirit, nor between body and soul, as many erroneously suppose, but between the lower self (the hylomorphic, composite self of the joint entity) and the higher or inner self. The goal of the soul's striving (including the soul of the athlete) is not so much a fundamental change in soul or an escape from the body as such as a waking up from illusion, a disciplined turning of one's attention from the lower to the higher or from the outer to the inner. Or again, the goal of *askesis* as athletic is nothing other than the ideal of *kalokagathia*.

Armstrong's translation of *askesis* as "training" accurately conveys in English the idea that asceticism is *for* something, as an athlete's disciplined training is only efficacious if it prepares the athlete for the competition. If the athlete wears the body out before the event, the athlete has not trained well. However, "discipline" can also, at times, be construed in a retributivist sense, which introduces too much negativity into Plotinian asceticism.

Plotinus uses the word *askesis* or its cognates at least five times.

1. At *Enneads* (1.1.10) Plotinus makes it clear that the joint entity—body and soul—is such that the soul cannot help but be affected by what happens to the body. The virtues (*aretai*) that result not from thought (*phronesei*) but from habit (*ethesi*) and training (*askesesi*) belong to the joint entity. Thus, virtue is obtainable by the joint entity (*koinon*), but only through training.

2. Just as some skills require arithmetic, so ethics (*ethon*) requires dialectic (*dialektikes*). But dialectic, although a necessary condition for an ethical life, is not sufficient (1.3.6). In addition one needs both contemplation (*theorousa*) and physical training (*askeseis*) in order to live the good life.

3. We should not be surprised that there are virtues associated with intellect that do not much involve the body and its athletic training (*askesei*). We can legitimately infer here (6.8.6) that the joint entity as knower cannot quite merge with the object of its quest. That is, although the highest religious vision in Plotinus at least partially or vicariously transcends the joint entity, it is nonetheless true that ascetic discipline is preparatory for such a vision.

4. By way of contrast, in Plotinus's opinion, Epicurus forfeits his banquet "there" in favor of one "here" (2.9.15). By exhorting us to pursue pleasure and to laugh at self-control (*sophronein*), on Plotinus's tendentious interpretation of Epicurus, the latter compromises the righteousness that we possess at birth and can have perfected by reason and athletic

training (*teleioumenen ek logou kai askeseos*). Thus, asceticism is not an artificial contrivance, but an extension of our natural predisposition to achieve *arete*. It does little good to suggest that we are to look to the higher life unless we are taught how to look. Only those trained to be passive in the right way are receptive to divine influence, just as the best athletes are those who anticipate the moves of another athlete in a contest. Trained passivity is a refined activity.

5. For Plotinus, human beings occupy a middle place (*metaxy*) between the gods and the animals; corrupted human beings pull themselves down to the level of wild beasts (*therion*). These corrupt human beings are obviously inferior, but this does not necessarily mean that Plotinus is opposed to the body or its training (3.2.8). Dainty children who are trained neither in bodily nor mental toughness are inferior to those chaotic souls who have at least trained (*askesantes*) their bodies. The training ground (*gymnasion*) of the latter has provided some means to combat laziness and luxury so as to secure moderation, as opposed to allowing human bodies to become "fattened lambs." Armstrong rightly notes that Plotinus is here criticizing a cowardly religiosity whereby people expect the gods to get them out of trouble when their proper task is to make themselves fit to handle such trouble. Nonetheless, Plotinus avoids the vice of taking asceticism too seriously. The wrestling schools (*palaistrai*) should be places for play. Analogously, simple (ascetic) meals can be quite enjoyable once pleonexic desires have been trimmed through training (Armstrong in Plotinus 1966–1988, 3:72–73).

Plotinus's allusions to athletics and his use of athletic metaphors amplify his specific uses of *askesis*. Like Herakles we must use our bodies in an active, not purely contemplative, life (1.1.12). It is the excellence (*arete*) of this active life to raise our ordinary nature (*koinon tes physeos*) to a higher level, standing up to the blows of fortune (*tyches*) like a great athlete (*athleten megan*). The very word "ethics" in English is derived from a Greek word for training or habit that is closely related to *askesis*: *ethos*. It is unfortunate that this connection has so infrequently been noticed. Plotinus makes it clear that the soul must be trained (*ethisteon*) in order to ascend (1.4.8, 1.6.7, 1.6.9). That is, even in Plotinus, who is often mistakenly thought of as advocating the flight of the soul away from the body, the ascetic life of athletic training and the ethical life are closely intertwined.

Four points should thus be emphasized: (1) *askesis* and *ethos*, and hence athletic discipline and ethics, are not as different as is normally assumed; (2) there is an athletic origin to both of these terms; hence, (3) there need not be anything morbid or life denying about either asceticism or ethics, in that athletics can be life affirming; and (4) both athletic discipline and ethics involve a certain dynamism as the exercitant asymptotically approaches the goal of athletic and/or spiritual (or ethical) "victory."

Like those who receive inherited wealth, some are naturally virtuous; others achieve intellectual virtue largely without the body, presumably because of a dispositional indifference to it. But most can achieve virtue only by first producing bodily vigor (*somatos ischyn*). In that the world is like a playing field (*gymnasion*), where some win and some lose, we should not be surprised that many people do not make the ascent to virtue. But to *fear* that we are to be among the losers creates a self-fulfilling prophecy because the winners are those, prepared by nature and training (*pareskeuasmenois physesi kai epimeleiais*), who draw near to the untroubled virtuous state (2.3.14; 2.9.9; 2.9.18).

Something similar to the Keating-like distinction between play and athletics is operative in Plotinus, with the former (from *paizo*) signifying children's games and the latter signifying a competition for a prize (from *athleo*), especially the aforementioned Olympia of the soul. *Askesis* does not have much to do with play *if* play is a mere trifling with toys (*paignia*), but to the extent that there is intrinsic, rather than merely instrumental, value in the asceticism practiced by the hylomorphic joint entity asceticism is not fully to be identified with a prize or some other effect (3.2.15). That is, in Huizinga-like and Feezell-like fashion there is no necessary opposition between play and athletics. In that *askesis* has elements of both intrinsic and instrumental value, there is a playful element in Plotinus's asceticism. In fact, he sees no danger in playing with one's own ideas (*kindynos oudeis en toi paizein ta auton genesetai*), as long as this playing (*paizein*) is ultimately for the sake of contemplation (*theorias*). A person who frivolously plays with ideas may unknowingly be training for the contemplative life (3.8.1), however—say, by getting the intellect used to its own work rather than exhausting it in utilitarian concerns.

Nonetheless, for the most part it is not play that improves us, but exercises (*meletai*) for the soul that are analogous to physical training (*gymnasia*) for the arms and legs. Just as physical training can be specialized, say, for a runner as opposed to a boxer, so can the soul's power be directed toward memory, or quick decisions, and so on. Proper training of the soul will insure that it will not be affected by distractions, just as a runner's training produces immunity to the pains of an otherwise demanding run (4.6.3). A quality like running or boxing is a power (*dynamis*) for Plotinus, which, when added to the *dynamis* of natural ability yields a greater sum than if the *dynamis* of natural ability were left on its own (6.1.10–12). Without an analogous power in the soul, the power that comes from training, we would more easily degenerate into vice, which for human beings largely consists in giving free reign to manifold desires (6.4.15).

Plotinus's way of life, as Robert Whittemore puts it, is a process of continuing discipline of body and mind directed to the goal of discovering the basic quality of nature and of self (Whittemore 1966). To be more precise, it is a training in preparation for finding out how our lives and nature are in God. Whatever we think of theism, however, should not get in the way of the realization that asceticism is anything but world negating, penitential, or mortifying (see Winkler and Cole 1994). Or again, to use the language of Heather Reid, the goal is to become "a philosophical athlete" (Reid 2002). This goal involves a parallelism between physical and intellectual exercises wherein both our bodies and our minds are transformed (see Hadot 1995, 59, 102, 111, 122, 136).

4. *HOMO LUDENS*, PROCESS, AND NARRATIVE

The process of becoming a virtuous athlete is illuminated not only by the Weissian quest for *arete* and the Plotinian emphasis on *askesis* and *ethos* as athletic, but also by the dynamism implicit in the *Homo ludens* hypothesis. Just as moral character is better judged in terms of virtuous habits built up over the course of time rather than in terms of performance in some in extremis situation, so also athletes are best judged—both as athletes and as persons—over the course of time rather than primarily in revenue-enhancing playoff games (Dixon 2002).

The processual nature of the *Homo ludens* hypothesis becomes most apparent in its connection to a theory of narration. Athletics not only gives us a momentary reprieve from quotidian reality; it also helps to give shape to our lives in general. As Feezell puts the twofold point: "First, sport provides the occasion for intrinsically interesting experiences, and insofar as it does, is aesthetically valuable. Second, sport also provides contexts for meaning for people, narratives that become existentially valuable for selves seeking a sense of meaning in life" (Feezell 2004a, 33). One can agree with Feezell here without going so far as to say that life itself is absurd. Further, in this quotation one can see the two sorts of process found in athletics as noticed by Wertz: atomic and transitional.

Life need not be, and ideally is not, just "one damned thing after another," as the misleading cliché has it. That is, the stories that we tell about our lives need not be arbitrary or mendacious or both. For example, we judge biographies of great athletes in terms of their accuracy to the facts. Or again, the events in one's life are misunderstood if they are seen as strictly externally related to each other in Humean fashion such that any order among them is a likely story that is no better or worse than any other tale we might tell. The time of our lives is asymmetrical: we are internally related to our pasts, but externally related to "our" futures. Each person's past supplies necessary, although not sufficient, conditions for everything that that person does. The sufficient conditions, which are not "mapped out" or "in the cards" beforehand, are supplied by our own de-cisions (literally, the cutting off of some possibilities and the preservation of some others).

It is noteworthy that Feezell sides here with (the process philosopher) John Dewey rather than with (the existentialist) Jean-Paul Sartre. The latter *does* seem to think that life is one damned thing after another. It is not even a tale told by an idiot in that it is not really a narrative tale (Feezell 2004a, 36). For Dewey, however, the present athlete contains his or her past. What a baseball pitcher is able to do in the fourth inning *depends on* whether he or she has established a fastball in the first three innings. But what is actually done in the fourth inning (which cannot be predicted in any detail, only anticipated) adds novelty to the game. Granted, if a pitcher *never* throws a breaking ball when behind in the count, the game is not as novel as it could be, but who knows with absolute assurance and in minute detail beforetime how well the opposing batters will hit this pitcher (Dewey 1958; Sartre 1964)?

Just as there is a narrative structure to games, so also there is a narrative structure to human (or sentient) life in general. The importance of the issue at hand will become apparent if Feezell is correct in his claim that "I can think of no area in modern life (except watching television, I suppose) that offers more possibilities for storylike experiences than sports" (Feezell 2004a, 43–44). Athletic contests, he thinks, help many people to keep the wolf of despair at bay: "If our gods are dead, our politics shallow, our cultural life thin, our work alienated, and our relation to the world overly technological, we may need the atmosphere of play and narrative more than ever. (The overcommercialization of sport may be cause for despair as well.)" (Feezell 2004a, 44). Athletic play (or spectatorship) enables one, however trivially, to *care* about something.

In addition to judging narratives against the standard of accuracy, we also morally judge the subjects of the narratives themselves. The criteria here, if the subject of the narrative in question is an athlete, are familiar. Athletic strength of character involves responding well to negative events, especially defeat in crucial games. We are apt to notice the absence of this quality in whiners like Kobe Bryant. Strength of character also involves the avoidance of cheating, the ability to get along with others (especially in team athletics), and an effort to understand athletic narratives in the context of more weighty metanarratives (Feezell 2004a, 139–140).

One once again wonders regarding such weighty metanarratives how far the comparison between athletics and tragedy can be pushed. Clearly there are certain similarities. In each there is a plot that involves struggle (*agon*) and dramatic tension; each involves loss that is often due to a fatal flaw (*hamartia*); this loss often occurs after a reversal (*peripeteia*) that makes possible, but does not guarantee, recognition (*anagnorisis*) of what has happened and why, a recognition that can bring about a release of intense emotion (*catharsis*); and both envelop all of the above in grand spectacle, as in the ancient entrance tunnel (*kryptos esodos*) and its contemporary foggy counterpart.

These similarities, ably studied by Francis Keenan (Keenan 1973), only tell part of the story, not quite half of it, in my estimation. Athletics is at least partially separate from the rest of life, existing in a splendid triviality, to use Feezell's language. That is, athletic loss is relatively trivial, in contrast to egregious suffering or premature death. An athlete's *life* can be tragic, but not qua his or her status as athlete, unless, of course, the egregious suffering or premature death is brought about in an athletic contest itself, as in Darryl Stingley's case. This is why I earlier argued against the absurdity of (weighty) life in contrast to the absurdity of (relatively trivial) athletics. If athletics is play, it might contribute to overall happiness (*eudaimonia*), but it is not to be identified with it (Fink 1974).

5. MCNAMEE AND OLYMPISM

The process of becoming virtuous as an athlete that I am examining in this chapter obviously bears a resemblance not only to the "aretism" of Weiss, but also to that of Holowchak and Reid in contemporary philosophy of athletics. Further, it is very much like the contemporary "Olympism" of Mike McNamee and other scholars. By this latter word is meant a modified version of the previously treated view of athletic competition that comes from de Coubertin. Integral to this view is the encouragement to seek balance between mind and body as encapsulated in the ideal of *kalokagathia*. And integral to the process of reaching this ideal is a certain joy in the spirit of competition itself. McNamee rightly eschews any essentialist definition of "Olympism" and instead tries to understand its various meanings and uses, which bear a Wittgensteinian family resemblance to each other. However, these meanings and uses all seem to involve a sense of fair play or sportsmanship. ("Sportspersonship" would be better, if it were not so cumbersome, in that it is gender inclusive.) We have seen that Feezell helps us to understand the concept of sportsmanship in Aristotelian terms that still have resonance in the twenty-first century.

A virtue ethics that has its roots in ancient Greek philosophy can help to underwrite contemporary Olympism by clarifying and encouraging certain agent-centered properties that are widely, if not universally, seen as desirable in athletes: courage, competitiveness, yet also fairness and sportsmanship. In several excellent articles McNamee alerts us to the obstacles to such an underwriting: virtues flourish in (MacIntyre-like) practices, but it is often difficult (yet required) to distinguish between athletic practices (e.g., running, basketball) and the bureaucratic institutions (e.g., the International Olympic Committee, the NBA) that nurture and/or corrupt them; individual pursuit of virtue is sometimes (often?) inundated with social pressures that overwhelm it; the distinction between internal and external goods sometimes breaks down as these two categories interpenetrate with each other; and there is no algorithm for determining how many athletic virtues there are, whether some athletic virtues are more important than others, or whether the virtues in question are universal (McNamee 2006, 174–180).

McNamee's intuitions, it seems to me, are almost always right when confronting these problems. For example, we can start with the conviction that the aforementioned deception and simulation that characterized the 2006 World Cup in soccer (e.g., faking injury to gain a strategic advantage) indicate that something is terribly wrong with contemporary athletics. But this conviction should not reify into a dogmatic stance when it is realized that athletic virtues vary somewhat from one historical era to another and from one culture to another. We really do not expect soccer and baseball superstars to possess the modesty of sumo wrestlers, on McNamee's helpful example. But this legitimate point can easily be overemphasized. The Japanese hitter Ichiro Suzuki is my favorite baseball player at present both because of his incredible baseball talent (offensively and defensively) *and* because of his modesty, a quality that reminds me of the American player Stan Musial from a previous generation. That is, it seems that *some* version of sportsmanship is crucial in *any* version of athletics. McNamee notes, however, that "in the UK at least, home to the Victorian legacy of moralistic sports and the muscular Christianity that so inspired de Coubertin, it was always thought that somehow, magically, the very playing of sports would inculcate in its practitioners moral qualities we think of as virtues. Nothing, it strikes me, warrants such confidence" (McNamee 2006, 185). I agree. But the inference to draw here is not that sportsmanship is to be trivialized, but that sportsmanship as moderation between the serious and the nonserious is to be approached processually: gradually, with stops and starts and temporary setbacks and with much effort.

Sportsmanship seems to transcend not only cultural boundaries, but temporal ones as well, as the present book is intended to illustrate. The usurpation of the internal goods of athletics by external ones was not foreign to ancient athletics. The task for us today, as it was for the ancient Greeks, is to find the proper balance of internal and external goods. For example, those who applaud athletics because of its ability to foster character development (a goal external to athletic activity itself) often fail to notice that athletics is also a breeding ground for vice. There is also the question of whether activities that are propaedeutic to athletic competition (e.g., weight training, aerobic conditioning) are goods that are internal to athletics or external to it (albeit as a type of preathletic activity rather than as an extraathletic activity). In any event, not all external goods corrupt the internal ones; for example, money allows one to become a professional athlete so as to, at least in principle, pursue bodily excellence without the fear of falling into poverty as a result, contra de Coubertin (McNamee 1995; Morgan 1994).

Olympism depends not so much on amateurism in the sense of not getting paid for one's athletic activity, as de Coubertin thought, as on the concept of *honor*. (In a different sense, we have seen that even paid athletes can be amateurs in the literal sense of their loving their games.) As McNamee again insightfully puts the point, "conceptions of honorable conduct are always in the background, with attendant virtues and vices" (McNamee 2002, 39). The distant historical horizon of the background mentioned here includes the agonal myths of the ancient Greeks, many of which were deadly. But I have held throughout the book that athletics is the Jamesian moral equivalent of war rather than an Orwellian war minus the shooting. If honor is crucial to the aretic or Olympian view of athletics, however, one must also face up to the fact that humiliation is possible. I do not have in mind humiliation in the strong sense wherein one's very personhood is disrespected (this should always be avoided), but in a weaker sense wherein one experiences shame, say, when one loses badly due to mental error and has to "bite the dust" or the humus (which provides the root meaning of "humility" as well as "human"). Feezell distinguishes between these two by calling the latter "embarrassment" and only the former "humiliation." Weak humiliation is made more likely by hubris, where the prideful individual acts as if it is impossible that he or she loses badly. But losing badly is always a possibility, even for an excellent athlete, as reflective competitors have always realized. "The broad-chested swagger of hubris still is as vicious now as it was in the days of Agamemnon" (McNamee 2002, 50; also Feezell 2004a, 120–121; Sessions 2004).

A wiser course of action, as McNamee rightly argues, is to see athletic greatness as on loan from the gods. Both athletic victories and defeats are only temporary. This transitoriness mirrors the ongoing process of trying to *understand* athletic victories and defeats, both ancient and contemporary, and of trying to shape contemporary views of athletics by pointing toward certain ideals that can act as lures or enticements to a better athletic world. This would be a world that would be both egalitarian and aretic. All who wish to participate in athletics should be allowed, indeed encouraged, to do so, yet the best athletes should be acknowledged as such (see DaCosta 2006; Parry 2006).

6. REFLECTIVE EQUILIBRIUM

Throughout the book I have been guided by the idea that an adequate philosophy of athletics would include a careful consideration of several ancient Greek ideals, especially as discussed by Plato, Aristotle, and Plotinus. The ancient Greek ideals that have been my foci (*arete, dynamis, sophrosyne, askesis, paidia,* and *kalokagathia*) are, I have argued, efficacious standards to keep in mind in the effort to understand what athletics is or ought to be. Further, Weiss, Huizinga, and Feezell (along with many other insightful writers in the contemporary world, especially McNamee) enable us to see what athletics could still contribute to the process of becoming virtuous. It will be the purpose of this final section to emphasize the reflective equilibrium that would be required among these various ideals and theories in an adequate philosophy of athletics.

A reflective person clearly wants to avoid both taking athletics too seriously (as did the fan during the 2002 World Cup in soccer who set himself on fire so as to rally his team to victory) and not taking it seriously enough (say, by allowing external goods to dominate athletics). A related distinction is that between one's subjective seriousness about athletics and the relative nonseriousness of it when viewed objectively. Without necessarily subscribing to William Morgan's criticisms of Feezell's views, it is nonetheless astute of Morgan to notice that reflective equilibrium is an *intersubjective* practice. The subjects in question—ancient and contemporary—each have something to say that ought not to be ignored. Or better, we ignore what they say at our peril. The process of becoming a virtuous athlete, fan, or coach is often facilitated by a consideration of the dynamism among the ancient Greek ideals themselves and among the various thinkers exemplifying these ideals in contemporary philosophy. And we should not give up on the hope that some sort of overlapping consensus might emerge in this dynamic process of trying to reach reflective equilibrium. For example, Weiss, Huizinga, and Feezell all agree with the claims made in the first two sentences of the present paragraph (Morgan 2007).

Current athletic practice is one factor among many that must be considered, but when other factors are put into play there is no guarantee that current practice will be rationally defensible, as Morgan correctly notes. For example, as a result of the argumentation in this book I think it is fair to say that the enormous role that money plays in contemporary athletics, and not merely at the professional level (French 2004), ought not to be accepted without question; indeed, such a muscular role unfortunately tends to deemphasize or even to corrupt the many internal goods of athletics, which are more numerous than even Aristotle could have imagined (see Suits 2007, 17). A social world without athletics would be an impoverished one for a "sports nut" like myself, but I very often wish it were a different social world from the one we have at present, one with fewer monetary concerns, fewer steroids, fewer maniacal viewers of athletic events (although not necessarily fewer viewers), fewer enticements to give in to blind patriotism in international competitions, and fewer philosophically unreflective commentators on athletics (Morgan 2002a, 2002b).

These negative points suggest, by way of contrast, several positive ones that could be made. As a result of the argumentation in this book, it makes sense to work toward, or at least to hope for, a closer connection between athletics and the life of virtue (*arete*); a more moderate (i.e., sophrosynic) approach to athletics in contrast to the vices of excessive seriousness in athletics and the trivialization of athletics; a more reflective approach to the active and passive power (*dynamis*) of the athletic body; a more frank and intelligent appreciation for the ascetic life; and, most importantly, a greater appreciation for the *Homo ludens* hypothesis and the ideal of *kalokagathia*, where virtues of the body and those of the mind are cultivated in harmony with each other.

The method of reflective equilibrium is Aristotelian and Rawlsian not only in its opposition to dogmatism (each plausible view deserves a hearing and defensible points from all quarters deserve inclusion in any adequate philosophy of athletics), but also in its possible contribution to a just democratic society. Reasonable adjudication of conflicting claims just *is* what a just society is all about. It is not unreasonable to hope that athletic competition could play a constructive role in the effort to bring about a just society, as it did in part in the nascent democracy in ancient Athens. That is, athletic competition is a prime example of nonviolent conflict resolution (assuming Parry's definitions of "aggression" and "violence"). For example, the Olympic movement at its best, both in the ancient world and in our own, can contribute to international peace. More generally, however, is the idea integral to literal competition that to lose an athletic event is not to become a "loser." Frans De Wachter argues that it is not accidental that modern athletics was born in another nascent democracy, nineteenth-century England, where conflicts among various people were, at least in theory, to be resolved according to "a sense of fair play" and by "playing within the rules." These phrases are now commonplaces in democracies largely due to athletics, it should be noted (De Wachter 2002).

One learns to peacefully accept opposition in both athletics and democracy, just as one learns to delegate authority to an adjudicator who is, once again in theory, neutral: a referee or a judge. One is reminded here of the ancient use of the *rhabdos* and its role in the development of equality under the law (*isonomia*). It did not escape Rawls's own notice that fair political procedures are facilitated by inculcation via games. Like winning an athletic event, winning an election is a transitory victory that still leaves us all with the processual project of trying to gradually work for justice (De Wachter 2002; Rawls 1999a, 409, 460–461).

Rawls is instructive, however, not only regarding the method of reflective equilibrium, in general, but also regarding the application of this method to athletics, in particular. He notes four related facets of games, in general, and athletic games, in particular, that are ideally in harmony with each other. These are (1) the desire to win the game, say, by scoring the most runs; (2) the "excitement" that comes from the playing of the game itself; (3) social purposes served by the game, which may or may not be known by the participants; and (4) a type of cooperative "social union" created when the game is played well by "good sports" (Rawls 1999a, 409, 460–461). The second facet has a family resemblance to the ludic approach to athletics, and the fourth facet points us once again toward the positive role that athletics to some extent does play, but to a greater extent could play, in a society that approximates justice. Or again, because Rawls sees baseball as a "higher" pleasure in John Stuart Mill's sense of the term, he implies that athletic activity can be autotelic as well as instrumental in the process of moving to a just society. Nonetheless, I would be remiss if I did not also call attention to the fact that Rawls is (unfortunately) helpful regarding nonideal conditions in athletics. These tend to occur when the parties involved have too much information and tendentiously try to advance their sides by cheating or by trying to force their views on others. The Rawlsian veil of ignorance often enables us to deal fairly with these cases in ways that might not otherwise be possible (Rawls 2007, 17–18, 307).

Both athletic contests and democracy are practices defined by rules. Without the rules of baseball, for example, one could run ninety feet, but one could not steal a base; without laws in a democratic society, one could give speeches, but one could not win an election. Starting at the associational level of children's athletic teams, ideally one learns to play fairly and to accept the outcome of games, just as ideally one learns to accept the outcome of fair votes. Or again, ideally one learns not to protest against there being different positions on the field (pitcher, shortstop), along with their privileges and powers, just as ideally one learns about the roles of president and senator. These privileges and powers are accepted as long as they are won in a fair competition, although in both athletics and politics it is at times understandable to think that the losers deserved to win. Athletic cheating and tax fraud are quintessential violations of the duty of fair play, a duty that is owed primarily to fellow players and citizens rather than to referees or government officials.

The point here is that, in addition to the intrinsic value of joyful play in athletic events, implied by both Rawls and Thomas Aquinas, and without which these events would not be what they are, there is the important instrumental value that comes from the realization that a just society is like a fair game. In both cases we at least tacitly, and at times explicitly, agree to play by the rules. This instrumental value is present even if there exist those whose worldview is centered around aesthetic values and repose in nature, and hence who fail to appreciate (or who even detest) competitive adventure (see Rawls 1999a, 485; 1999b, 20, 31, 37–38, 50, 61, 75, 99, 102, 117–129, 150, 190, 195–197, 209–214, 381, 468). Further, to admit the possibility of the instrumental value that athletics could have for fair decision-making procedures in politics is not exactly to claim to have an insider's advantage regarding *the* good, concerning which there are significant disagreements in a democratic society.

The pitfalls are numerous in the efforts to understand what athletics is and ought to be. For example, I have tried to avoid the romantic tendency to fuse a description of ancient athletics with what ought to exist in the twenty-first century. The ideals that I have been concerned with in this book provided a *horizon* for ancient thinkers, rather than a realized utopia, just as they could provide the same for us. In some ways the ancients were closer to these ideals than we are, and in other ways they were further from them (as in the denigration of women and slaves as not worthy of athletics). A helpful example of the former tendency, however, is provided by Reid: "To the ancients, an Olympic victory was imagined as a visit from the winged goddess *Nike*, who swooped down from Olympus to briefly bless the mortal athlete with a divine crown of sacred olive. To us moderns, Olympic victory is more likely to be associated with Nike, the multinational megacompany, which swoops down from Wall Street to briefly bless the athlete with a fat paycheck and temporary status as a corporate shill" (Reid 2006b, 205). If our society is at base commercial, the ancient Greek one was at its core religious. I am a romantic at least to the extent that I see this transition as regressive. However, athletes can still at times be literally inspired (breathed into by something or someone greater than themselves). Luckily for us they can also at times be inspiring (see Burkert 1985).

Along with George Santayana we are philosophers "on the bleachers." Perhaps we are "fans," too, but the fact that this word is a shortened version of "fanatics" should give us pause. "Spectator" avoids this difficulty, but the ocular distance implied in this word does not seem to do enough to capture the extent to which we are invested in the athletic contests we watch. In addition, the fact that athletics is, according to Santayana, probably more Spartan than it is Athenian should prepare us for the likelihood that most athletes, coaches, and fans will not easily warm up to philosophical approaches to athletics. We should also expect the trivialization of athletics on the part of fellow philosophers concerned with more meaty topics (or, in some instances, supposedly more meaty topics).

I hope I have shown, however, that the topic of contemporary athletics and ancient Greek ideals is hardly thin gruel. At the very least it points us toward a play world that could or does exist as a "promising rebellion" against excessive gravitas. In any event, the conclusion I have defended that we ought not to take athletics too seriously should help to fend off philosophers who would otherwise sneer at philosophy of athletics (Santayana 1972).

Those who take contemporary athletics and ancient Greek ideals seriously are also held in check by the ancient sources themselves. Cornford is correct to remind us that the mythic origin of the Olympic Games found in the story of Pelops and Oinomaos involves a contest between the young and the old that concerns who should be king; their race is for the kingdom itself. But one can be "king" only for a limited time after an athletic victory. The fact that the Olympic crown of victory was made of transitory olive branches rather than metal symbolizes the fact that victory is but a moment in the overall process of becoming virtuous. Always we have before us (literally for Pelops, metaphorically for contemporary athletes) the task of how to become a king (*basileus*). More precisely, because the very earliest races at Olympia were among virgins who were dedicated to Hera, it would perhaps be more accurate to speak of the temporary monarchy, rather than the temporary kingship, of a victorious athlete, who must eventually abdicate the throne in that even athletic dynasties terminate and even the best athletic bodies deteriorate (Cornford 1927).

In one sense, each day is the same in that we always face the same questions: how to be just? how to be wise? The method of reflective equilibrium is such that important philosophical responses to these questions offered by utilitarians, deontologists (e.g., Brown 2003; Feezell 2004b), and social contract theorists, among others, contain important insights that ought not to be ignored. But the agent-centered dimension of judgments we make in athletics is also crucial (e.g., McNamee and Jones 2003). Indeed, this dimension is more prominent here than in almost any other area, presumably because of the logic of athletic competition itself, where the pursuit of winged victory puts intense, public pressure on the competitors themselves to be fair, sportsmanlike, and graceful even in defeat. (By contrast, a professor's failures in the classroom, committee room, or library are rarely made known to a wide public.) This pressure is precisely what makes the process of becoming virtuous in athletics so interesting and so difficult.

Bibliography

Algozin, Keith. 1976. "Man and Sport." *Philosophy Today* 20:190–195.

Angell, Roger. 1985. "The Interior Stadium." In *Sport Inside Out: Readings in Literature and Philosophy*, ed. Spencer Wertz and David Vanderwerken. Fort Worth: Texas Christian University Press.

Anscombe, G. E. M. 1958. "Modern Moral Philosophy." *Philosophy* 33:1–19.

Arieti, James. 1975. "Nudity in Greek Athletics." *Classical World* 68:431–436.

Aristotle. 1934. *The Nicomachean Ethics*. Trans. Harris Rackham. Loeb Classical Library. Cambridge, MA: Harvard University Press.

———. 1984. *The Complete Works of Aristotle*. Ed. Jonathan Barnes. 2 vols. Princeton: Princeton University Press.

Armstrong, A. H. 1940. *The Architecture of the Intelligible Universe in the Philosophy of Plotinus*. Cambridge: Cambridge University Press.

Arnold, Peter. 2002. "Three Approaches toward an Understanding of Sportsmanship." In *Philosophy of Sport*, ed. Andrew Holowchak. Upper Saddle River, NJ: Prentice-Hall.

Barthes, Roland. 2007. *What Is Sport?* Trans. Richard Howard. New Haven: Yale University Press.

Bergmann, Frithjof. 1977. *On Being Free*. Notre Dame: University of Notre Dame Press.

Bergmann Drewe, Sheryle. 2001. *Socrates, Sport, and Students*. Lanham, MD: University Press of America.

Best, David. 2002. "The Aesthetic in Sport." In *Philosophy of Sport*, ed. Andrew Holowchak. Upper Saddle River, NJ: Prentice-Hall.

Blackburn, Simon. 2000. "Enquivering." *New Republic*, October 30, 43–48.

Brown, W. M. 2003. "Personal Best." In *Sports Ethics*, ed. Jan Boxill. Oxford: Blackwell.

Burckhardt, Jacob. 1999. *The Greeks and Greek Civilization*. Trans. Oswyn Murray. London: St. Martin's.

Burfoot, Amby. 2002. "White Men Can't Run." In *Philosophy of Sport*, ed. Andrew Holowchak. Upper Saddle River, NJ: Prentice-Hall.

Burkert, Walter. 1985. *Greek Religion*. Trans. John Raffan. Cambridge, MA: Harvard University Press.

Caillois, Roger. 1961. *Man, Play, and Games*. Trans. Meyer Barash. New York: Free Press.

Camus, Albert. 1955. *The Myth of Sisyphus*. Trans. Justin O'Brien. New York: Vintage Books.

Caputo, John. 1997. *The Prayers and Tears of Jacques Derrida*. Bloomington: Indiana University Press.

Carr, David. 2002. "Where's the Merit If the Best Man Wins?" In *Philosophy of Sport*, ed. Andrew Holowchak. Upper Saddle River, NJ: Prentice-Hall.

Cordner, Christopher. 2002. "Differences between Sport and Art." In *Philosophy of Sport*, ed. Andrew Holowchak. Upper Saddle River, NJ: Prentice-Hall.

Corlett, John. 2002. "Virtue Lost: Courage in Sport." In *Philosophy of Sport*, ed. Andrew Holowchak. Upper Saddle River, NJ: Prentice-Hall.

Cornford, F. M. 1927. "The Origin of the Olympic Games." In *Themis*, ed. Jane Harrison. Cambridge: Cambridge University Press.

Crowther, Nigel. 1984. "Studies in Greek Athletics." *Classical World* 78:497–558.

———. 1985. "Studies in Greek Athletics." *Classical World* 79:73–135.

———. 1999a. "Athlete as Warrior in the Ancient Greek Games." *Nikephoros* 12:121–130.

———. 1999b. "The Finish in the Greek Foot-Race." *Nikephoros* 12: 131–142.

DaCosta, Lamartine. 2006. "A Never-Ending Story: The Philosophical Controversy over Olympism." *Journal of the Philosophy of Sport* 33: 157–173.

De Coubertin, Pierre. 2000. *Olympism: Selected Writings*, ed. Norbert Muller. Lausanne: International Olympic Committee.

De Wachter, Frans. 2002. "Education for Peace in Sports Education." In *Philosophy of Sport*, ed. Andrew Holowchak. Upper Saddle River, NJ: Prentice-Hall.

Dewey, John. 1958. *Art as Experience*. New York: Capricorn Books.

Diogenes Laertius. 1950. *Lives of Eminent Philosophers*. Trans. R. D. Hicks. Cambridge: Harvard University Press.

Dixon, Nicholas. 1992. "On Sportsmanship and 'Running Up the Score.'" *Journal of the Philosophy of Sport* 19:1–13.

———. 2002. "On Winning and Athletic Superiority." In *Philosophy of Sport*, ed. Andrew Holowchak. Upper Saddle River, NJ: Prentice-Hall.

———. 2007. "Trash Talking, Respect for Opponents and Good Competition." *Sport, Ethics and Philosophy* 1:96–106.

Dombrowski, Daniel. 1979. "Plato and Athletics." *Journal of the Philosophy of Sport* 6:29–38.

———. 1987. "Asceticism as Athletic Training in Plotinus." *Aufstieg und Niedergang der Romischen Welt* 36, no. 1:701–712.

———. 1990. "Two Vegetarian Puns at *Republic* 372." *Ancient Philosophy* 9:167–171.

———. 1991. *Christian Pacifism*. Philadelphia: Temple University Press.

———. 1995. "Weiss, Sport, and the Greek Ideal." In *The Philosophy of Paul Weiss*, ed. Lewis Hahn. Chicago: Open Court.

———. 2001. *Rawls and Religion: The Case for Political Liberalism*. Albany: State University of New York Press.

———. 2002. "Rawls and War." *International Journal of Applied Philosophy* 16:185–200.

———. 2004. *Divine Beauty: The Aesthetics of Charles Hartshorne*. Nashville: Vanderbilt University Press.

———. 2005. *A Platonic Philosophy of Religion: A Process Perspective*. Albany: State University of New York Press.

———. 2006. *Rethinking the Ontological Argument: A Neoclassical Theistic Response*. New York: Cambridge University Press.

Drees, Ludwig. 1968. *Olympia: Gods, Artists, and Athletes*. Trans. Gerald Onn. New York: Praeger.

Ehman, Robert. 1970. Review of *Sport: A Philosophic Inquiry*, by Paul Weiss. *Dialogue* 8:750–753.

Eitzen, D. Stanley. 2002. "The Dark Side of Competition." In *Philosophy of Sport*, ed. Andrew Holowchak. Upper Saddle River, NJ: Prentice-Hall.

English, Jane. 1978. "Sex Equality in Sports." *Philosophy and Public Affairs* 7:269–277.

Esposito, Joseph. 1988. "Play and Possibility." In *Philosophic Inquiry in Sport*, ed. William Morgan and Klaus Meier. Champaign, IL: Human Kinetics.

Feezell, Randolph. 1981a. "Sport: Pursuit of Bodily Excellence or Play? An Examination of Paul Weiss's Account of Sport." *Modern Schoolman* 58:257–270.

———. 1981b. "Play, Freedom, and Sport." *Philosophy Today* 25:166–175.

———. 1984. "Play and the Absurd." *Philosophy Today* 28:319–329.

———. 1986. "Sportsmanship." *Journal of the Philosophy of Sport* 13:1–13.

———. 1988. "On the Wrongness of Cheating and Why Cheaters Can't Play the Game." *Journal of the Philosophy of Sport* 15:57–68.

———. 1989. "Sport, Character, and Virtue." *Philosophy Today* 33: 204–220.

———. 1995. "Sport, the Aesthetic, and Narrative." *Philosophy Today* 39:93–104.

———. 1999. "Sportsmanship and Blowouts: Baseball and Beyond." *Journal of the Philosophy of Sport* 26:68–78.

———. 2001. "Sport and the View from Nowhere." *Journal of the Philosophy of Sport* 28:1–17.

———. 2004a. *Sport, Play, and Ethical Reflection*. Chicago: University of Illinois Press.

———. 2004b. "Baseball, Cheating, and Tradition: Would Kant Cork His Bat?" In *Baseball and Philosophy*, ed. Eric Bronson. Chicago: Open Court.

————. 2005. "Celebrated Athletes, Moral Exemplars, and Lusory Objects." *Journal of the Philosophy of Sport* 32:20–35.

Feezell, Randolph, and Craig Clifford. 1997. *Coaching for Character*. Champaign, IL: Human Kinetics.

Feezell, Randolph, and William Stephens. 2004. "The Ideal of the Stoic Sportsman." *Journal of the Philosophy of Sport* 31:196–211.

Feinberg, Joel. 1984. "Absurd Self-Fulfillment." In *Philosophy and the Human Condition*, ed. Tom L. Beauchamp, William T. Blackstone, and Joel Feinberg. Englewood Cliffs, NJ: Prentice-Hall.

Fink, Eugen. 1974. "The Ontology of Play." *Philosophy Today* 18:147–161.

Finley, M. I., and H. W. Pleket. 1976. *The Olympic Games: The First Thousand Years*. New York: Viking Press.

Foot, Philippa. 2003. *Virtues and Vices*. Oxford: Oxford University Press.

Fraleigh, Warren. 1988. "Why the Good Foul Is Not Good." In *Philosophic Inquiry in Sport*, ed. William Morgan and Klaus Meier. Champaign, IL: Human Kinetics.

Frankl, Viktor. 1978. *The Unheard Cry for Meaning*. New York: Simon and Schuster.

French, Peter. 2004. *Ethics and College Sports*. Lanham, MD: Rowman and Littlefield.

Fry, Jeffrey. 2004. "Sports and 'The Fragility of Goodness.'" *Journal of the Philosophy of Sport* 31:34–46.

Gaffney, Paul. 2006. "In the Zone: How the Confident Athlete Exemplifies Aristotelian Virtue." Paper delivered at the American Philosophical Association Convention, Washington, DC.

Gardiner, E. N. 1930. *Athletics of the Ancient World*. Oxford: Oxford University Press.

Geach, Peter. 1977. *The Virtues*. Cambridge: Cambridge University Press.

Golden, Mark. 1998. *Sport and Society in Ancient Greece*. Cambridge: Cambridge University Press.

————. 2004. *Sport in the Ancient World from A to Z*. New York: Routledge.

Gough, Russell. 1997. *Character Is Everything: Promoting Ethical Excellence in Sports*. New York: Harcourt Brace College.

Guardini, Romano. 1997. *The Spirit of the Liturgy*. Trans. Ada Lane. New York: Crossroad.

Habicht, Christian. 1999. *Pausanias' Guide to Ancient Greece*. Berkeley: University of California Press.

Hadot, Pierre. 1995. *Philosophy as a Way of Life*. Trans. Michael Chase. Oxford: Blackwell.

Hardie, W. F. R. 1968. *Aristotle's Ethical Theory*. Oxford: Clarendon Press.

Harris, H. A. 1964. *Greek Athletes and Athletics*. London: Hutchinson.

Hartshorne, Charles. 1973. *Born to Sing*. Bloomington: Indiana University Press.

Holowchak, Andrew. 1996. "The Early Greek Influence on Sport: Legendary Figures of Greek Sport." *Milo* 4:44–46.

———. 2002a. "Moral Liberalism and the Atrophy of Sport." In *Philosophy of Sport*, ed. Andrew Holowchak. Upper Saddle River, NJ: Prentice-Hall.

———. 2002b. "'Aretism' and Pharmacological Ergogenic Aids in Sport." In *Philosophy of Sport*, ed. Andrew Holowchak. Upper Saddle River, NJ: Prentice-Hall.

———. 2004. *Happiness and Greek Ethical Thought*. New York: Continuum.

Huizinga, Johan. 1955. *Homo Ludens: A Study of the Play-Element in Culture*. Trans. R. F. C. Hull. Boston: Beacon Press.

———. 1996. *The Autumn of the Middle Ages*. Trans. Rodney Payton and Ulrich Mammitzsch. Chicago: University of Chicago Press.

Hundley, Joan. 2002. "The Overemphasis on Winning: A Philosophical Look." In *Philosophy of Sport*, ed. Andrew Holowchak. Upper Saddle River, NJ: Prentice-Hall.

Hursthouse, Rosalind. 1999. *On Virtue Ethics*. Oxford: Oxford University Press.

Hyland, Drew. 1977. "'And That Is the Best Part of Us': Human Being and Play." *Journal of the Philosophy of Sport* 4:36–49.

———. 1984. *The Question of Play*. Lanham, MD: University Press of America.

———. 1990. *Philosophy of Sport*. New York: Paragon House.

Ignatius of Loyola, St. 1951. *The Spiritual Exercises of St. Ignatius*. Trans. Louis Puhl. Chicago: Loyola University Press.

Jackson, Phil. 1995. *Sacred Hoops*. New York: Hyperion.

James, William. 1984. "The Moral Equivalent of War." In *The Essential Writings*, ed. Bruce Wilshire. Albany: State University of New York Press.

Jeu, Bernard. 1972. "What Is Sport?" *Diogenes* 80:150–163.

Kaelin, E. F. 2002. "The Well-Played Game." In *Philosophy of Sport*, ed. Andrew Holowchak. Upper Saddle River, NJ: Prentice-Hall.

Keating, James. 1964. "Sportsmanship as a Moral Category." *Ethics* 75: 25–35.

Keenan, Francis. 1973. "The Athletic Contest as a 'Tragic' Form of Art." In *The Philosophy of Sport*, ed. Robert Osterhoudt. Springfield, IL: Charles Thomas.

Kennell, Nigel. 1995. *The Gymnasium of Virtue: Education and Culture in Ancient Sparta*. Chapel Hill: University of North Carolina Press.

Kidd, Bruce. 2002. "The Men's Cultural Centre: Sports and the Dynamic of Women's Oppesssion/Men's Repression." In *Philosophy of Sport*, ed. Andrew Holowchak. Upper Saddle River, NJ: Prentice-Hall.

Kretchmar, R. Scott. 1995. "From Test to Contest: An Analysis of Two Kinds of Counterpoint in Sport." In *Philosophic Inquiry in Sport*, 2nd ed., ed. William Morgan and Klaus Meier. Champaign, IL: Human Kinetics.

———. 2005. *Practical Philosophy of Sport and Physical Activity*. 2nd ed. Champaign, IL: Human Kinetics.

Kuntz, Paul. 1976. "Paul Weiss: What Is Philosophy of Sport?" *Philosophy Today* 20:170–189.

———. 1977. "Paul Weiss on Sports as Performing Arts." *International Philosophical Quarterly* 17:147–165.

Kyle, Donald. 1987. *Athletics in Ancient Athens*. Leiden: Brill.

Lasch, Christopher. 1979. *The Culture of Narcissism*. New York: Warner Books.

Lee, Hugh. 1983. "Athletic Arete in Pindar." *Ancient World* 7:31–37.

Lehman, Craig. 2002. "Can Cheaters Play the Game?" In *Philosophy of Sport*, ed. Andrew Holowchak. Upper Saddle River, NJ: Prentice-Hall.

Lenk, Hans. 1979. *Social Philosophy of Athletics*. Champaign, IL: Stipes Publishing.

————. 1985. "Herculean 'Myth' Aspects of Athletics." In *Sport Inside Out: Readings in Literature and Philosophy*, ed. Spencer Wertz and David Vanderwerken. Fort Worth: Texas Christian University Press.

Lewandowski, Joseph. 2007. "Boxing: The Sweet Science of Constraints." *Journal of the Philosophy of Sport* 34:26–38.

Liddell, Henry, and Robert Scott. 1996. *A Greek-English Lexicon*. New York: Oxford University Press.

Loland, Sigmund. 2002. "Fair Play: Historical Anachronism or Topical Ideal?" In *Philosophy of Sport*, ed. Andrew Holowchak. Upper Saddle River, NJ: Prentice-Hall.

MacAloon, John. 1981. *This Great Symbol: Pierre de Coubertin and the Origins of the Modern Olympic Games*. Chicago: University of Chicago Press.

MacIntyre, Alasdair. 1984. *After Virtue*. 2nd ed. Notre Dame: University of Notre Dame Press.

Mandell, Richard. 1987. *The Nazi Olympics*. Chicago: University of Illinois Press.

Martinkova, Irena. 2001. "*Kalokagathia*: How to Understand Harmony of a Human Being." *Nikephoros* 14:21–28.

Matz, David. 1991. *Greek and Roman Sport: A Dictionary of Athletes and Events from the Eighth Century B.C. to the Third Century A.D.* Jefferson, NC: McFarland.

McBride, Frank. 1979. "Toward a Non-definition of Sport." In *Sport and the Body*, 2nd ed., ed. Ellen Gerber and William Morgan. Philadelphia: Lea and Febiger.

McNamee, Mike. 1995. "Sporting Practices, Institutions, and Virtues." *Journal of the Philosophy of Sport* 22:61–82.

————. 2002. "Hubris, Humility, and Humiliation: Vice and Virtue in Sporting Communities." *Journal of the Philosophy of Sport* 29:38–53.

————. 2006. "Olympism, Eurocentricity, and Transcultural Virtues." *Journal of the Philosophy of Sport* 33:174–187.

————. 2007. "Whose Prometheus? Transhumanism, Biotechnology and the Moral Topography of Sports Medicine." *Sport, Ethics and Philosophy* 1:181–194.

McNamee, Mike, and Carwyn Jones. 2003. "Moral Development and

Sport: Character and Cognitive Developmentalism Contrasted." In *Sports Ethics*, ed. Jan Boxill. Oxford: Blackwell.

Meier, Klaus. 2002. "Triad Trickery: Playing with Sports and Games." In *Philosophy of Sport*, ed. Andrew Holowchak. Upper Saddle River, NJ: Prentice-Hall.

Midgley, Mary. 1974. "The Game Game." *Philosophy* 49:231–253.

Mihalich, Joseph. 1982. *Sports and Athletics: Philosophy in Action*. Totowa, NJ: Rowman and Littlefield.

Miller, Stephen. 2004a. *Ancient Greek Athletics*. New Haven: Yale University Press.

———. 2004b. *Arete: Greek Sports from Ancient Sources*. Berkeley: University of California Press.

Morgan, William. 1977. "Some Aristotelian Notes on the Attempt to Define Sport." *Journal of the Philosophy of Sport* 4:15–35.

———. 1994. *Leftist Theories of Sport*. Chicago: University of Illinois Press.

———. 2002a. "Sport in the Larger Scheme of Things." In *Philosophy of Sport*, ed. Andrew Holowchak. Upper Saddle River, NJ: Prentice-Hall.

———. 2002b. "Sports and the Making of National Identities: A Moral View." In *Philosophy of Sport*, ed. Andrew Holowchak. Upper Saddle River, NJ: Prentice-Hall.

———. 2006. *Why Sports Morally Matter*. New York: Routledge.

———. 2007. "Why the 'View from Nowhere' Gets Us Nowhere in Our Moral Considerations of Sport." In *Ethics in Sport*, 2nd ed., ed. William Morgan. Champaign, IL: Human Kinetics.

Mosley, Albert. 2002. "Racial Differences in Sports." In *Philosophy of Sport*, ed. Andrew Holowchak. Upper Saddle River, NJ: Prentice-Hall.

Mumford, Stephen. 2007. "Virtue and Vice in Sport." Paper delivered at the British Philosophy of Sport Association Conference, Leeds.

Murdoch, Iris. 1971. *The Sovereignty of Good*. New York: Schocken Books.

Nagel, Thomas. 1979. "The Absurd." In *Mortal Questions*. New York: Cambridge University Press.

———. 1986. *The View from Nowhere*. New York: Oxford University Press.

Neils, Jennifer. 1998. "Games, Prizes, and Athletics in Greek Sports." *Classical Bulletin* 74:120–125.

Novak, Michael. 1976. *The Joy of Sport*. New York: Basic Books.

Nussbaum, Martha. 1986. *The Fragility of Goodness: Luck and Ethics in Greek Tragedy and Philosophy*. Cambridge: Cambridge University Press.

Olivova, Vera. 1984. *Sports and Games in the Ancient World*. New York: St. Martin's Press.

Orwell, George. 1968. *Collected Essays, Journalism and Letters*. Vol. 4. New York: Harcourt, Brace, and World.

Parry, Jim. 2002. "Violence and Aggression in Contemporary Sport." In *Philosophy of Sport*, ed. Andrew Holowchak. Upper Saddle River, NJ: Prentice-Hall.

———. 2006. "Sport and Olympism: Universals and Multiculturalism." *Journal of the Philosophy of Sport* 33:188–204.

Pausanias. 1979. *Description of Greece*. Trans. Peter Levi. 2 vols. New York: Penguin.

Phillips, David, and David Pritchard, eds. 2003. *Sport and Festival in the Ancient Greek World*. Swansea: Classical Press of Wales.

Pieper, Josef. 1979. "Play: A Non-meaningful Act." In *Sport and the Body*, 2nd ed., ed. Ellen Gerber and William Morgan. Philadelphia: Lea and Febiger.

Pindar. 2004. *Olympian Odes*. Trans. William Race. Athens: Greek Font Society.

Plato. 1977. *Opera*. Ed. John Burnet. 5 vols. Oxford: Clarendon Press.

———. 1999. *Collected Dialogues*. Ed. Edith Hamilton and Huntington Cairns. Princeton: Princeton University Press.

Plotinus. 1966–1988. *Enneads*. Trans. A. H. Armstrong. 7 vols. Loeb Classical Library. Cambridge: Harvard University Press.

Poliakoff, Michael. 1987. *Combat Sports in the Ancient World*. New Haven: Yale University Press.

Popper, Karl. 1979. *Objective Knowledge*. Oxford: Clarendon Press.

Porphyry. 1965. *On Abstinence from Animal Food*. Trans. Thomas Taylor. London: Centaur.

Postow, B. C. 2002. "Women and Masculine Sports." In *Philosophy of Sport*, ed. Andrew Holowchak. Upper Saddle River, NJ: Prentice-Hall.

Rahner, Hugo. 1965. *Man at Play*. New York: Herder and Herder.

Raschke, Wendy. Ed. 1988. *The Archeology of the Olympics*. Madison: University of Wisconsin Press.

Rawls, John. 1999a. *A Theory of Justice*. Rev. ed. Cambridge: Harvard University Press.

———. 1999b. *Collected Papers*. Ed. Samuel Freeman. Cambridge: Harvard University Press.

———. 2007. *Lectures on the History of Political Philosophy*. Ed. Samuel Freeman. Cambridge: Harvard University Press.

Reid, Heather. 2002. *The Philosophical Athlete*. Durham, NC: Carolina Academic Press.

———. 2003. "Plato." *Encyclopedia of Leisure and Outdoor Recreation*. London: Routledge: 373.

———. 2006a. "Was the Roman Gladiator an Athlete?" *Journal of the Philosophy of Sport* 33:37–49.

———. 2006b. "Olympic Sport and Its Lessons for Peace." *Journal of the Philosophy of Sport* 33:205–214.

———. 2007. "Sport and Moral Education in Plato's *Republic*." *Journal of the Philosophy of Sport* 34:160–175.

Riezler, Kurt. 1941. "Play and Seriousness." *Journal of Philosophy* 38: 505–517.

Roochnik, David. 1975. "Play and Sport." *Journal of the Philosophy of Sport* 2:36–44.

Rorty, Richard. 1979. *Philosophy and the Mirror of Nature*. Princeton: Princeton University Press.

Sansone, David. 1988. *Greek Athletics and the Genesis of Sport*. Berkeley: University of California Press.

Santayana, George. 1972. "Philosophy on the Bleachers." In *Sport and the Body*, ed. Ellen Gerber. Philadelphia: Lea and Febiger.

Sartre, Jean-Paul. 1964. *Nausea*. Trans. Lloyd Alexander. New York: New Directions.

Scanlon, Thomas. 2002. *Eros and Greek Athletics*. Oxford: Oxford University Press.

Schacht, Richard. 1973. "On Weiss on Records, Athletic Activity and the Athlete." In *The Philosophy of Sport*, ed. Robert Osterhoudt. Springfield, IL: Charles Thomas.

Schmitz, Kenneth. 1979. "Sport and Play: Suspension of the Ordinary." In *Sport and the Body*, 2nd ed., ed. Ellen Gerber and William Morgan. Philadelphia: Lea and Febiger.

Segal, Erich. 1967. "It Is Not Strength, but Art, Obtains the Prize." *Yale Review* 56:606–608.

Sessions, William. 2004. "Sportsmanship as Honor." *Journal of the Philosophy of Sport* 31:47–59.

Simon, Robert. 1984. "Good Competition and Drug-Enhanced Performance." *Journal of the Philosophy of Sport* 11:289–296.

———. 1985. *Sports and Social Values*. Englewood Cliffs, NJ: Prentice-Hall.

———. 2002. "Sportsmanship and Fairness in the Pursuit of Victory." In *Philosophy of Sport*, ed. Andrew Holowchak. Upper Saddle River, NJ: Prentice-Hall.

———. 2007. "Deserving to Be Lucky: Reflections on the Role of Luck and Desert in Sports." *Journal of the Philosophy of Sport* 34:13–25.

Sinn, Ulrich. 2000. *Olympia: Cult, Sport, and Ancient Festival*. Princeton: Wiener.

Slote, Michael, and Roger Crisp, eds. 1997. *Virtue Ethics*. Oxford: Oxford University Press.

Spelman, Elizabeth. 1995. "Woman as Body: Ancient and Contemporary Views." In *Philosophic Inquiry in Sport*, 2nd ed., ed. William Morgan and Klaus Meier. Champaign, IL: Human Kinetics.

Spivey, Nigel. 2004. *The Ancient Olympics: A History*. Oxford: Oxford University Press.

Suits, Bernard. 1967. "What Is a Game?" *Philosophy of Science* 34:148–156.

———. 2002. "Tricky Triad: Games, Play, and Sport." In *Philosophy of Sport*, ed. Andrew Holowchak. Upper Saddle River, NJ: Prentice-Hall.

———. 2007. "The Elements of Sport." In *Ethics in Sport*, 2nd ed., ed. William Morgan. Champaign, IL: Human Kinetics.

Swaddling, Judith. 1999. *The Ancient Olympic Games*. Austin: University of Texas Press.

Sweet, Waldo. 1987. *Sport and Recreation in Ancient Greece*. New York: Oxford University Press.

Tamburrini, Claudio. 2002. "Sports, Fascism, and the Market." In *Philosophy of Sport*, ed. Andrew Holowchak. Upper Saddle River, NJ: Prentice-Hall.

Tannsjo, Torbjorn. 2002. "Is Our Admiration for Sports Heroes Fascistoid?" In *Philosophy of Sport*, ed. Andrew Holowchak. Upper Saddle River, NJ: Prentice-Hall.

Thomas Aquinas, St. 1972. *Summa Theologiae*. Ed. Blackfriars. New York: McGraw-Hill.

Ullian, Joseph. 1973. "Review of Paul Weiss, *Sport: A Philosophic Inquiry*." *Journal of Philosophy* 70:299–301.

Vasari, Giorgio. 1957. *Lives of the Artists*. Trans. E. L. Seeley. New York: Noonday.

Veblen, Thorstein. 1934. *The Theory of the Leisure Class*. New York: Modern Library.

Walzer, Michael. 2000. *Just and Unjust Wars*. 3rd ed. New York: Basic Books.

Warnock, G. J. 1971. *The Object of Morality*. London: Methuen.

Weiss, Paul. 1969. *Sport: A Philosophic Inquiry*. Carbondale: Southern Illinois University Press.

———. 1971. *Philosophy in Process*. Vols. 1, 5. Carbondale: Southern Illinois University Press.

———. 1973. "Records and the Man." In *The Philosophy of Sport*, ed. Robert Osterhoudt. Springfield, IL: Charles Thomas.

———. 1980. "Games: A Solution to the Problem of the One and the Many." *Journal of the Philosophy of Sport* 7:7–14.

———. 1981. "The Nature of a Team." *Journal of the Philosophy of Sport* 8:47–54.

———. 1982. "Some Philosophical Approaches to Sport." *Journal of the Philosophy of Sport* 9:90–93.

———. 1995a. "Reply to Daniel A. Dombrowski." In *The Philosophy of Paul Weiss*, ed. Lewis Hahn. Chicago: Open Court.

———. 1995b. "Reply to S. K. Wertz." In *The Philosophy of Paul Weiss*, ed. Lewis Hahn. Chicago: Open Court.

Wertz, Spencer. 1991. *Talking a Good Game: Inquiries into the Principles of Sport*. Dallas: Southern Methodist University Press.

———. 1995. "The Metaphysics of Sport: The Play as Process." In *The Philosophy of Paul Weiss*, ed. Lewis Hahn. Chicago: Open Court.

———. 2002. "Is Sport Unique? A Question of Definability." In *Philosophy of Sport*, ed. Andrew Holowchak. Upper Saddle River, NJ: Prentice-Hall.

Whitehead, Alfred North. 1925. *Science and the Modern World*. New York: Macmillan.

———. 1978. *Process and Reality*. Corrected ed. New York: Free Press.

Whittemore, Robert. 1966. "Panentheism in Neo-Platonism." *Tulane Studies in Philosophy* 15:47–70.

Winkler, Mary, and Letha Cole, eds. 1994. *The Good Body: Asceticism in Contemporary Culture*. New Haven: Yale University Press.

Wordsworth, William. 1981. *Poetical Works*. Oxford: Oxford University Press.

Young, David. 1984. *The Olympic Myth of Greek Amateur Athletics*. Chicago: Ares.

Index